# Daily Dev
# Inspired Word of God

### A 365 Day Devotional of
### Patterns Truths and Inspirations

by J. Gordon Monson

*Danny + Debbie*

*Jim Monson*

While every precaution has been taken in the preparation of this book, the publisher assumes no responsibility for errors or omissions, or for damages resulting from the use of the information contained herein.

DAILY DEVOTIONAL WITH THE INSPIRED WORD OF GOD

**First edition. November 12, 2021.**

Copyright © 2021 J. Gordon Monson.

ISBN: 979-8201512507

Written by J. Gordon Monson.

# Acknowledgements:

These one liners were written after almost four decades of Bible (NKJV) studies, along with sitting under the teachings of earlier pastors, Elmore Heitman, Gilbert Delao, Curtiss Paul.

Then more resent pastors, Greg Phelps, William Del Casale, Justin Morris, Ali Reza Abbassi, Bob Fitzgerald, Tim Jenks, Toby Beck, Matt Daniells and Ryan Aufemkamp. Some of these pastors remain an ongoing source of study, encouragement, and inspiration helping me to write even more one liners.

Others who've given me ideas for the one liners come from presentations and talks from such notable people as the late Sir Winston Churchill, along with a few former U. S. Presidents, including President Trump, and from some other National current and former elected officials.

Other sources are from good friends and close relatives who have inspired me with deep, meaningful conversations over the years. These are almost too many to list them all, but I will give you my short list: My brother, Ronald and his wife, Pauline Monson, My wife and best friend, Clarice Monson, who has been my greatest inspiration in all that I do. My sister, Cheryl Monson Jerome and her husband, Jerry Jerome, who now live just under an hour away from us. My Late Brother, Dennis Eugene Monson, and his dear wife, Dorothy Monson, both who are now gone to be with the Lord, along with my older sister, JoAnne Monson Skramstad, all of who continue to encourage and challenged me with their strong faith in the Lord during their last years. My sweet daughter, Teresa Monson Nyswonger, and my two granddaughters, Talon and Taylor, along with my grandson, Jared Monson Conway and his dear Mother, Odette Monson Conroy, and her family are always a good source of encouragement. My good friends, Drew Lee, Jay Gross, Fred Morgan, Jr., Brian Anderson, and Al McKnight, along with so many other close Christian friends who have been a blessing to me both now and over these many years of Christian fellowship.

The last, but certainly not the least, is the Lord Jesus Christ, who is my Savior, my Redeemer and my Soon Coming King. He has never left me. He is always with me, and He has promised to soon come back for His Church, of which I am so thankful to be a part. He has asked us to remain ready for His soon coming, in a day and hour which none of us knows. But, He tells us He will come back in a day when we least expect His return.

DAILY DEVOTIONAL WITH THE INSPIRED WORD OF GOD 3

## Instructions and consent/comments:

You have the right to make this book you are now holding your daily source for your devotions. You can personalize this book with your additions to all of the 365 or 366 (leap year) subjects. Like the Lord says, "No two of us are exactly alike." You can put (your take) on any one of these subjects. How you do it is also up to you. I plan to use this as a part of my daily studies. I will be putting down some of my own "Your takes," as I go through this devotional each day of the year.

Life changes, different events, and how I might feel when I go to read each will likely change from year to year. It may even help many of those coming behind us when they read what we added for the various subjects at different times in our life.

You can order this book in printed format as well as eBook. Whether you choose to order your Daily Devotional in eBook or in a printed copy format you will need a separate journal to add (Your take.) You can do this either in separate written journal, or in the notes file of your device. How you do this is up to you. I like to write the devotional number, the subject of the one liner, and then the date followed by (my take) for each day of the year in a comment or with your selection of Bible verse of your choosing.

# The first one liner is taken from the Book of Genesis:

1. In the beginning God created the heavens and the earth. He didn't like the darkness and void so He said "Let there be light." Then He saw that it was good.

   Genesis 1: 1 - 4a In the beginning God created the heavens and the earth. The earth was without form, and void; and darkness was on the face of the deep. And the Spirit of God was hovering over the face of the waters. Then God said, "Let there be light"; and there was light. And God saw the light that it was good.

   (Add (YOUR TAKE) in a separate written journal or in the notes file on your device:)


2. On day six God created man in His own image.
   Genesis 1:27 So God created man in His own image; in the image of God He created him; male and female He created them.
   Colossians 1:16 For by Him all things were created that are in heaven and earth, visible, whether thrones or dominions or principalities or powers. All things were created through Him and for Him.
   Your Take:


3. Truthfulness always prevails in the end.
   Psalms 25:5 Lead me in Your truths and teach me, for You are the God of my salvation; on You I wait all the day.
   John 14:6 Jesus said to him, "I am the way, the truth, and the life. No on comes to the Father except through Me."
   Your take:

4. Knowledge and wisdom are two different conditions.

Psalms 94:10 He who instructs the nations, shall He not correct, He who teaches man knowledge?

Romans 11:33 Oh, the depth of the riches both of the wisdom and knowledge of God! How unsearchable are His judgements and His ways past finding out.

( My take: (Paraphrase: ) Knowledge is the storage of information, while wisdom it the best use of that knowledge.

Your take:

5. Planning ahead saves time, money, and nerves, almost without fail.

Ephesians 1:11 In Him also we have obtained an inheritance, being predestined according to the purpose of Him who works all things according to the counsel of His will, that we who first trusted in Christ should be to the praise of His glory.

Your take:

6. Retain and nurture old friendships, and encourage new ones as well.

Proverbs 12:26 The righteous should choose his friends carefully, for the way of the wicked leads them astray.

1 John 4:7 Beloved, let us love one another, for love is of God; and everyone who loves is born of God and knows God.

Your take:

7. Never compromise beyond your moral and spiritual values.

Proverbs 10: 2 – 4 Treasures of the wicked profit nothing, but righteousness delivers from death. The Lord will not allow the righteous soul to famish, but He casts away the desire of the wicked. He who has a slack hand becomes poor, but the hand of the diligent makes rich.

Colossians 2:23 These things indeed have an appearance of wisdom in self-imposed religion, false humility, and neglect of the body, but are of no value against the indulgence of the flesh.

Your Take:


8. Health and wealth may help promote happiness, but are not a requirement, happiness is a state of mind.

Ecclesiastes 3:1 – 4 To everything there is a season, a time for every purpose under heaven: A time to be born, and a time to die; a time to plant, and a time to pluck what is planted; a time to kill, and a time to heal; a time to break down, and a time to build up; a time to weep, and a time to laugh; a time to mourn, and a time to dance.

James 5:13 Is anyone among you suffering? Let him pray. Is anyone among you cheerful? Let him sing psalms.

Your take:


9. To have a friend one must be a good friend.

Proverbs 16:32 He who is slow to anger is better than the mighty, and he who rules his spirit than he who takes a city.

Romans 12:21 Do not be overcome by evil, but overcome evil with good.

Your take:


10. Always schedule proper rest in each twenty four hour day.

Genesis 2:2 And on the seventh day God ended His work which He had done, and He rested on the seventh day from all His work which He had done.

Matthew 11:28 Come to Me, all you who labor and are heavy laden, and I will give you rest.
Your take:




11. The pursuit of great wealth may lead to jealousy, while the pursuit of great integrity leads to admiration.
Psalm 7:8 The Lord shall judge the people; judge me, O Lord, according to my righteousness, and according to my integrity within me.
Titus 2:6 – 8 Likewise, exhort the young men to be sober-minded, in all things showing yourself to be a pattern of good works; in doctrine showing integrity, reverence, incorruptibility. Sound speech that cannot be condemned, that one who is an opponent may be ashamed, having nothing evil to say of you.
Your take:




12. With the world going to the dogs, buy stock in dog food companies.
Zechariah 11:12 – 13 Then I said to them, "If it is agreeable to you, give me my wages; and if not, refrain." So they weighed out for my wages thirty pieces of silver. And the Lord said to me, "Throw it to the potter" – that princely price they set on me. So I took the thirty pieces of silver and threw them into the house of the Lord for the potter.
1 Corinthians 6:20 For you were bought at a price, therefore glorify God in your body and in your spirit, which are God's.
Your take:


13. Always speak the truth, and expect the same from others.
Psalm 119:30 I have chosen the way of truth; Your judgements I have laid before me.

John 3:21 But he who does the truth comes to the light, that his deeds may be clearly seen, that they have been done in God.

Your take:

14. Those willing to eat last may one day be brought to the front of the line.

Matthew 19:29 – 30 And everyone who has left houses or brothers or sisters or fathers or mothers or wife or children or lands, for My sake, shall receive a hundredfold, and inherit eternal life. But many who are first will be last, and the last first.

Your take:

15. Make a will and update it every couple of years.

Genesis 15:3 Then Abram said, "Look, you have given me no offspring; indeed one born in my house is my heir!"

Galatians 4:1 Now I say that the heir, as long as he is a child, does not differ at all from a slave, though he is master of all, but is under guardians and stewards until such time appointed by the father.

Your take:

16. Three daily balanced meals helps to promote quality of life now and later.

Proverbs 15:17 Better is a dinner of herbs where love is, than a fatted calf with hatred.

Acts 10:14 – 15 But Peter said, "Not so Lord! For I have never eaten anything common or unclean. And a voice spoke to him again the second time, "What God has cleansed you must not call common."

Your take:


17. Be willing to go the extra mile.

Matthew 5:41 – 42 And whoever compels you to go one mile, go with him two. Give to him who asks you, and from him who wants to borrow from you do not turn away.

Your take:

18. Displayed trustworthiness will gain other's trust.

Proverbs 11:13 A talebearer reveals secrets, but he who is of a faithful spirit conceals a matter.

2 Timothy 2:11 This is a faithful saying: For if we died with Him, we shall also live with Him.

Your take:

19. Remember, you are part of God's creation; all appreciation, all glory and honor goes to Him.

Psalm 69: 34 – 35 Let heaven and earth praise Him, the seas and everything that moves in them. For God will save Zion and build the cities of Judah, that they may dwell there and possess it.

Jude 24 Now to Him who is able to keep you from stumbling, and to present you faultless before the presence of His glory with exceeding joy, to God our savior Who alone is wise, be glory and majesty, dominion and power, both now and forever. Amen.

Your take:

20. Be flexible, while always trying to keep good time management.

Genesis 26: 4 – 5 "I will make your descendants multiply as the stars of heaven; I will give to your descendants all these lands; and in your seed all the nations of the earth shall be blessed because Abraham obeyed My voice and kept My charge, My commandments, My statutes and My laws."

Matthew 4: 23 And Jesus went about all Galilee teaching in their synagogues, preaching the gospel of the kingdom, and healing all kinds of diseases among the people.

Your take:

21. Remember to hug your family every day.

Exodus 34:6 And the Lord passed before him and proclaimed, "The Lord, the Lord God, merciful and gracious, longsuffering, and abounding in goodness and truth, keeping mercy for thousands, forgiving iniquity, and transgression and sin, by no means clearing the guilty, visiting the iniquity of the fathers upon the children's children to the third and fourth generation."

1 Corinthians 13: 13 And now abide faith, hope, love, these three, but the greatest of these is love.

Your take:

22. Live each day as if it was your very last.

Psalm 1: 6 For the Lord knows the way of the righteous, but the way of the ungodly shall perish.

Romans 13:11 - 14 And do this, knowing the time, that now it is high time to awake out of sleep; for now our salvation is nearer than when we first believed. The night is far spent, the day is at hand. Therefore let us cast off the works of darkness, and let us put on the armor of light. Let us walk properly, as in the day, not in revelry and drunkenness, not in lewdness and lust, not in strife and envy. But put on the Lord Jesus Christ, and make no provision for the flesh, to fulfill its lusts.

Your take:

23. Avoid being wasteful and recycle whatever you can.

Matthew 26: 12 "For the pouring this fragrant oil on My body she did it for My burial."

John 6:12 So when they were filled, He said to His disciples, "Gather up the fragments that remain, so that nothing is lost."

Your take:

24. Regard work as an opportunity and challenge, not an obstacle and problem.

Proverbs 12:14 A man will be satisfied with good by the fruit of his mouth, and the recompense of a man's hands will be rendered to him.

Matthew 5: 16 Let your light so shine before men, that they may see your good works and glorify your Father in heaven.

Your take:

25. An active mind is rarely bored.

Ecclesiastes 2:24 Nothing is better for a man than that he should eat and drink, and that his soul should enjoy good in his labor. This also, I saw was from the hand of God.

Isaiah 26: 3 – 4 You will keep him in perfect peace, whose mind is stayed on You. Trust in the Lord forever, for in Yah, the Lord, is everlasting strength.

Your take:

26. Take time to get to know your neighbors.

Proverbs 3: 29 – 30 Do not devise evil against your neighbor, for he dwells by you for safety sake. Do not strive with a man without cause, if he has done you no harm.

1 John 1:7 But if we walk in the light as He is in the light, we have fellowship with one another, and the blood of Jesus Christ cleanses us from all sin.

Your take:

27. Butter your bread on only one side.

Proverbs 31:10 - 12 Who can find a virtuous wife? For her worth is far above rubies. The heart of her husband safely trusts her; so he will have no lack of gain. She does him good and not evil all the days of her life.

Luke 11: 3 – 4 "Give us day by day our daily bread. And forgive us our sins, for we also forgive everyone who is indebted to us. And do not lead us into temptation, but deliver us from the evil one."

Your take:

28. Be a good listener, listening with both ears.

John 9: 35 – 36 Jesus heard that they had cast him out; and when He had found him, He said to him, "Do you believe in the Son of God?" He answered and said, "Who is He Lord, that I may believe in Him?"

James 1:19 So then, my beloved brethren, let every man be swift to hear, slow to speak and slow to wrath; for the wrath of man does not produce the righteousness of God.

Your take:

29. Do something nice for someone every day.

Psalm 112:9 He has dispersed abroad, he has given to the poor; his righteousness endures forever; his horn will be exalted with honor.

1 Timothy 6:18 - 19 Let them do good, that they be rich in good works, ready to give, willing to share, storing up for themselves a good foundation for the time to come, that they may lay hold on eternal life.

Your take:

30. Honor God, Flag, and Country.

Colossians 3:16 – 17 Let the word of Christ dwell in you richly in all wisdom, teaching and admonishing one another in psalms and hymns and spiritual songs, singing with grace in your hearts to the Lord. And whatever you do in word and deed, do all in the name of the Lord Jesus, giving thanks to God the Father through Him.

Your take:

31. A brisk walk in fresh air clears the mind, relaxes the body and renews the spirit.

Proverbs 3: 23 – 24 Then you will walk safely in your way, and your foot will not stumble. When you lie down and you will not be afraid; yes, you will lie down and your sleep will be sweet.

Your take:

32. Tell your family every day that you love them.

Joshua 2:12 – 13 "Now therefore, I beg you, swear to me by the Lord, since I have shown you kindness, that you also will show kindness to my father's house, and give me a true token, and spare my father, my mother, my brothers, my sisters, and all that they have, and deliver our lives from death."

Your take:

33. Make others around you feel important.

Mark 8:2 - 3 "I have compassion on the multitude, because they have now continued with Me three days and have nothing to eat. And if I send them away hungry to their own houses, they will faint on the way; for some of them have come from afar."

Your take:

34. Mow in squares, not in circles.

Ezekiel 36:34 The desolate land shall be tilled instead of lying desolate in the sight of all who pass by. So they will say, "This land that was desolate has become like the Garden of Eden; and the wasted desolate, and ruined cities are now fortified and inhabited.'

Your take:

35. Don't be afraid to ask for clear directions.

1 Corinthians 12: 3 Therefore, I make known to you that no one speaking by the Spirit of God calls Jesus accursed, and no one can say that Jesus is Lord except by the Holy Spirit.

Your take:

36. Look for the good in each person.

Galatians 6: 4 – 5 But, let each one examine his own work, and then he will have rejoicing in himself alone, and not in another. For each one shall bear his own load.

Luke 12: 43 – 44 Blessed is that servant whom his master will find so doing when he comes. "Truly, I say to you that he will make him ruler over all that he has."

Your take:

37. Build bridges, not barriers.

Ephesians 4: 25 Therefore, putting away lying, "Let each one of you speak truth with his neighbor, for we are members of one another."

Galatians 6: 10 Therefore, as we have opportunity, let us do good to all, especially to those who are of the household of faith.

Your take:

38. Remember, you are not perfect yet, so don't expect perfection from others.

Philippians 3: 13- 14 Brethren, I do not count myself to have apprehended; But one thing I do, forgetting those things which are behind and reaching forward to those things which are ahead, I press toward the goal for the prize of the upward call of God in Christ Jesus.

Your take:

39. Work toward peace and co-operation whenever possible.

Psalm 34: 14 Depart from evil and do good; seek peace and pursue it.

Matthew 7: 12 Therefore, whatever you want men to do to you, do also to them, for this is the law and the prophets.

Your take:

40. Make God and your family first in your life.

Matthew 6: 32 – 34 For after all these things the Gentiles seek. For your heavenly Father knows that you need all these things. But seek first the kingdom of God and His righteousness, and all the things shall be added to you. Therefore do not worry about tomorrow, for tomorrow will worry about its own things. Sufficient for the day is its own trouble.

Hebrews 11: 7 By faith Noah, being divinely warned of things not yet seen, moved with godly fear, prepared an ark for the saving of his household, by which he condemned the world and became heir of the righteousness which is according to faith.

Your take:

41. Practice preventative maintenance daily.

Job 27:6 My righteousness I hold fast, and will not let it go; my heart shall not reproach me as long as I live.

1 John 3: 7 Little children, let no one deceive you. He who practices righteousness is righteous, just as He is righteous.

Your take:

42. Time wasted is lost forever.

Galatians 5: 13 – 14 For you brethren, have been called to liberty; only do not use liberty as an opportunity for the flesh, but through love serve on another. For all the law is fulfilled in one word, even in this: "You shall love your neighbor as yourself."

Your take:

43. A shady spot on a hot day is like a gift from above.

1 Kings 19: 5 – 6 Then as he (Elijah) lay and slept under a broom tree, suddenly an angel touched him, and said to him, "Arise and eat." Then he looked and there by his head was a cake baked on coals, and a jar of water.

Your take:

44. An orderly house is a reflection of its owners.

Proverbs 28: 6 Better is the poor who walks in his integrity than one perverse in his ways, though he be rich.

Ecclesiastes 12: 13 – 14 Let us hear the conclusion of the whole matter: Fear God and keep His commandments, for this is man's all. For God will bring every work into judgment, including every secret thing, whether good or evil.

Your take:

45. Time never stands still, so make the most of all you get.

Matthew 13: 11 – 14 He answered and said to them, "Because it has been given to you to know the mysteries of the kingdom of heaven, but to them it has not been given. For whoever has, to him more will be given, and he will have abundance; but whoever does not have, even what he has will be taken away from him. Therefore I speak to them in parables, because seeing they do not see, and hearing they do not hear, nor do they understand. And in them the prophecy of Isaiah is fulfilled, which says, 'Hearing you will hear and shall not understand, and seeing you will see and not perceive; for the hearts of this people have grown dull. Their ears are hard of hearing, and their eyes they have closed, lest they should see with their eyes and hear with their ears, lest they should understand with their hearts and turn, so that I should heal them.'

Your take:

46. Making memories is better than making money. Money and power are fleeting, but memories should last forever.

Isaiah 55: 2 – 4 Why do you spend money for what is not bread, and wages for what does not satisfy? Listen carefully to Me, and eat what is good, and let your soul delight itself in abundance. Incline your ear, and come to Me. Hear, and your soul shall live; and I will make an everlasting covenant with you – the sure mercies of David. Indeed I have given him as a witness to the people, a leader and commander for the people.

1 Thessalonians 4: 1 – 2 Finally then, brethren, we urge and exhort in the Lord Jesus that you should abound more and more, just as you received from us how you ought to walk and to please God; for you know what commandments we gave you through the Lord Jesus.

Your take:

47. A mean response just adds fuel to any quarrel.

Isaiah 32:17-18 The work of righteousness will be peace, and the effect of righteousness, quietness and assurance forever. My people will dwell in a peaceful habitation, in secure dwelling, and in quiet resting places.

James 1:19 So then, my beloved brethren, let every man be swift to hear, slow to speak, and slow to wrath; for the wrath of man does not produce the righteousness of God.

James 3:18 Now the fruit of righteousness is sown in peace by those who make peace.

Your take:

48. Always drink from a clean glass.

Matthew 23:26-27 Blind Pharisee, first cleanse the inside of the cup and dish, that the outside of them may be clean also. Woe to you, scribes and Pharisees, hypocrites! For you are like whitewashed tombs which indeed appear beautiful outwardly, but inside are full of dead men's bones and all uncleanness.

Luke 11:39-40 Then the Lord said to him, "Now you Pharisees make the outside of the cup and dish clean, but your inward part is full of greed and wickedness. Foolish ones! Did not He who made the outside make the inside also?"

Your take:

49. Take lots of pictures, they add to your memories.

Esther 9: 26 – 28 So they called these days Purim, after the name Pur. Therefore, because of all the words of this letter, what they had seen concerning this matter, and what had happened to them, the Jews established and imposed it upon themselves and their dependents and all who would join them, that without fail they should celebrate these two days every year, according to the written instructions and according to the prescribed time, that these days should be remembered and kept throughout every generation, every family, every province, and every city, that these days of Purim should not fail to be observed among the Jews, and that the memory of them should not perish among their descendants.

Your take:

50. Always strive to be courteous in whatever you do.

Titus 3: 1 - 2 Remind them to be subject to rulers and authorities, to obey, to be ready for every good work, to speak evil of no one, to be peaceable, gently, showing all humility to all men.

Your take:


51. Pause often to smell the roses.

Judges 19:9 And when the man stood to depart – he and his concubine and his servant – his father-in-law, the young woman's father, said to him, "Look the day is now drawing toward evening; please spend the night. See, the day is coming to an end; lodge here, that your heart may be merry. Tomorrow go your way early, so that you may get home."

Nehemiah 8:10 Then he said to them, "Go your way, eat the fat, drink the sweet, and send portions to those for who nothing is prepared; for this day is holy to our Lord. Do not sorrow, for the joy of the Lord is your strength."

Your take:

52. Strive to be on time, but always call if you are running late.

1Timothy 4:16 Take heed to yourself and to the doctrine. Continue in them, for in doing this you will save both yourself and those who hear you.

Your take:

53. Treat others like you'd like to be treated.

1Timothy 5: 1 - 3 Do not rebuke an older man, but exhort him as a father, younger men as brothers, older women as mothers, younger women as sisters, with all purity. Honor widows who are really widows.

1 Peter 3:7 Husbands, likewise, dwell with them with understanding, giving honor to the wife as to the weaker vessel, and as being heirs together of the grace of life, that your prayers may not be hindered.

Your take:

54. Share your blessings, and get an extra blessing just from the sharing.

1 Peter 3: 8 - 9 Finally, all of you be of one mind, having compassion for one another; love as brothers, be tenderhearted, be courteous; not returning evil for evil or reviling for reviling, but on the contrary blessing, knowing that you were called to this, that you may inherit a blessing.

Your take:

55. Set realistic goals, and then set about to achieve each.

Isaiah 65: 21 - 23 They shall build houses and inhabit them; they shall plant vineyards and eat their fruit. They shall not build and another inhabit; they shall not plant and another eat; for as the days of a tree, so shall be the days of My people, and My elect shall long enjoy the work of their hands. They shall not labor in vain, nor bring forth children for trouble; for they shall be the descendants of the blessed of the Lord and their offspring with them.

Your take:

56. Buy fruits and vegetables in their season.

Numbers 13: 23 - 25 Then they came to the Valley of Eshcol, and there cut down a branch with one cluster of grapes; they carried it between two of them on a pole. They also brought some of the pomegranates and figs. The place was called the Valley of Eshcol because of the cluster which the men of Israel cut down there. And they returned from spying out the land after forty days.

Your take:

57. Make plans for any future event.

Jerimiah 6: 4 - 5 Prepare war against her; arise, and let us go up at noon. Woe to us for the day goes away, for the shadows of the evening are lengthening. Arise, and let us go by night, and let us destroy her palaces.

Your take:


58. A cold drink helps to cool the body, and a glass of cold water also quenches one's thirst.

2 Samuel 23: 15 - 17 And David said with longing, "Oh, that someone would give me a drink of the water from the well of Bethlehem, which is by the gate!" So the three mighty men broke through the camp of the Philistines, drew water from the well of Bethlehem that was by the gate, and took it and brought it to David. Nevertheless he would not drink it, but poured it out to the Lord. And he said, "Far be it from me, O Lord, that I should do this! Is this not the blood of the men who went in jeopardy of their lives? Therefore he would not drink it. These things were done by the three mighty men.

Your take:

59. Be consistent in all good things you do.

1 Chronicles 29: 16 - 18 "O Lord our God, all this abundance that we have prepared to build You a house for Your holy name is from Your

hand, and is all Your own. I know also my God, that You test the heart and have pleasure in uprightness. As for me, in the uprightness of my heart I have willingly offered all these things; and now with joy I have seen Your people, who are present here to offer willingly to You. O Lord God of Abraham, Isaac, and Israel, our fathers, keep this forever in the intent of the thoughts of the heart of Your people, and fix their heart toward You."

Your take:

60. When all else fails, remember you should have prayed first.

2 Chronicles 7: 14 - 15 If My people who are called by My name will humble themselves, and pray, and seek My face, and turn from their wicked ways, then I will hear from heaven, and will forgive their sin and heal their land. Now My eyes will be open and My ears attentive to prayer made in this place.

Your take:

61. Home is where the heart is, and also where you began.

Mark 16: 19 - 20 So then, after the Lord had spoken to them, He was received up into heaven, and sat down at the right hand of God. And they went out and preached everywhere, the Lord working with them and confirming the word through the accompanying signs. Amen.

Your take:

62. Hug your family, lock the doors, turn off the lights, and then talk to the Lord at the end of each day.

Psalms 123: 3 - 4 Have mercy on us O Lord, have mercy on us! For we are exceedingly filled with contempt. Our soul is exceedingly filled with the scorn of those who are at ease. With the contempt of the proud.

Matthew 5: 44 – 45 But I say to you, love your enemies, bless those who curse you, do good to those who hate you, and pray for those who spitefully use you and persecute you, that you may be sons of your Father in heaven; for He makes His sun rise on the evil and on the good, and send rain on the just and on the unjust.

Your take:

63. Say 'Hello', it doesn't cost anything, and it just might brighten someone's day.

Genesis 12: 2 - 3 "I will make you a great nation; I will bless you and make your name great; and you shall be a blessing. I will bless those who bless you and curse him who curses you; and in you all the families of the earth shall be blessed."

Matthew 7: 24 - 25 Therefore whoever hears these saying of Mine, and does them, I will liken him to a wise man who built his house on the rock: and the rain descended, the floods came, and the winds blew and beat on that house; and it did not fall, for it was founded on the rock.

Your take:

64. The measure of a man should not be what he owns or how much power he has, but what he stands for.

Proverbs 31: 10 - 11 Who can find a virtuous wife? For her worth is far above rubies? The heart of her husband safely trusts her; so he will have no lack of gain.

1 Peter 3: 3 - 4 Do not let your adornment be merely outward-arranging the hair, wearing gold, or putting on fine apparel-but rather let it be the hidden person of the heart, with the incorruptible beauty of a gentle and quiet spirit, which is very precious in the sight of God.

Your take:

65. One lever properly placed moves more weight than several men can move without this aid.

Zechariah 4:9 "The hands of Zerubbabel have laid the foundation of this temple; his hands shall also finish it. Then you will know that the Lord of hosts has sent Me to you.

Colossians 4:17 And say to Archippus, "Take heed to the ministry which you have received in the Lord, that you may fulfill it."

Your take:

66. Accept changes when the benefits outweigh their drawbacks.

1 Samuel 16:1 Now the Lord said to Samuel, "How long will you mourn for Saul, seeing I have rejected him from reigning over Israel? Fill your horn with oil and go; I am sending you to Jesse the Bethlehemite. For I have provided Myself a king among his sons."

Your take:

67. Whatever you choose to do, do it with all of your effort.

Judges 16:30 Then Samson said, "Let me die with the Philistines!" And he pushed with all his might, and the temple fell on the lords and all the people who were in it. So the dead that he killed at his death were more than he had killed in his life.

Zechariah 4:6 So he answered and said to me: "This is the word of the Lord to Zerubbabel: Not by might nor by power, but by My Spirit, says the Lord of hosts.

Your take:

68. Who can know what will come tomorrow, but we should make preparation none-the-less.

Malachi 3:1 "Behold, I send My messenger, and he will prepare the way before Me. And the Lord, whom you seek, will suddenly come to His temple, even the Messenger of the covenant, in whom you delight. Behold, He is coming," says the Lord of hosts.

1 Peter 1: 13 - 16 Therefore gird up the loins of your mind, be sober, and rest your hope fully upon the grace that is to be brought to you at the revelation of Jesus Christ; as obedient children, not conforming

yourselves to the former lust, as in your ignorance, but as He who called you is holy, you also be holy in all your conduct, because it is written, "Be holy, for I am holy."

Your take:

69. If two is good, can three be better, maybe, but maybe not.

Numbers 22: 32 - 33 And the Angel of the Lord said to him, "Why have you struck your donkey these three times? Behold, I have come out to stand against you, because your way is perverse before Me. The donkey saw Me and turned aside from Me these three times. If she had not turned aside from Me, surely I would also have killed you by now, and let her live."

Your take:

70. God loves you and I should too.

Zephaniah 3:17 The Lord your God in your midst, The mighty One, will save; He will rejoice over you with gladness, He will quiet you with His love, He will rejoice over you with singing."

Mark 12: 30 - 31 And you shall love the Lord your God with all your heart, with all your soul, with all your mind, and with all your strength. This is the first commandment. And the second, like it, is this, you shall love your neighbor as yourself. There is no other commandment greater than these."

Your take:

71. No sincere act of kindness may go unnoticed, someday the reward will come.

Matthew 19: 29 - 30 And everyone who has left houses or brothers or sisters or father or mother or wife or children or lands for My name sake, shall receive a hundredfold, and inherit eternal life. But many who are first will be last, and the last first.

Mark 9: 35 - 37 And He sat down, called the twelve, and said to them, "If anyone desires to be first, he shall be last of all and servant of all." Then He took a little child and set him in the midst of them. And when He had taken him in His arms, He said to them, "Whoever receives one of these little children in My name receives Me; and whoever receives Me, receives not Me but Him who sent Me."

Your take:

72. Make time for family every day, the benefits will be worth the effort.

John 11: 42 - 43 And I know that You always hear Me, but because of the people who are standing by I said this, that they may believe that You sent Me. Now when He had said these things, He cried with a loud voice, "Lazarus, come forth!"

Ephesians 4:29 Let no corrupt word proceed out of your mouth, but what is good for necessary edification, that it may impart grace to the hearers.

Your take:

73. Work smarter, not harder.

Esther 9: 20 - 22 And Mordecai wrote these things and sent letters to all the Jews, near and far, who were in all the provinces of King Ahasuerus, to establish among them that they should celebrate yearly the fourteenth and fifteenth days of the month of Adar, as the days on which the Jews had rest from their enemies, as the month which was turned from sorrow to joy for them, and from mourning to a holiday; that they should make them days of feasting and joy, of sending presents to one another and gifts to the poor.

Your take:

74. Worship the Creator, not the created.

Joshua 22:29 "Far be it from us that we should rebel against the Lord, and turn from following the Lord this day, to build an altar for burnt offerings, for grain offerings, or for sacrifices, besides the altar of the Lord our God which is before His tabernacle."

Judges 6:10 Also I said to you, "I am the Lord your God; do not fear the gods of the Amorites, in whose land you dwell. But you have not obeyed My voice."

Your take:

75. A smile takes much less effort than a frown, so smile more and everyone benefits.

Psalm 126: 2 - 3 Then our mouth was filled with laughter, and our tongue with singing. Then they said among the nations, "The Lord has done great things for them. The Lord has done great things for us, and we are glad."

Proverbs 17:22 A merry heart does good, like medicine, but a broken sprit dries the bones.

Your take:

76. Clear, concise directions given help others to follow instructions.

2 Chronicles 35: 4 - 6 "Prepare yourselves according to your fathers' houses, according to your divisions, following the written instruction of David, king of Israel, and the written instruction of Solomon, his son. And stand in the holy place according to the divisions of the fathers' houses of your brethren the lay people, and according to the division of the father's house of the Levites. So slaughter the Passover offerings, consecrate yourselves, and prepare them for your brethren, that they may do according to the word of the Lord by the hand of Moses."

Your take:

77. Relax, life is too short to sweat the small stuff.

Hebrews 13: 5 – 6 Let your conduct be without covetousness; be content with such things as you have. For He Himself has said, "I will never leave you nor forsake you." So we may boldly say: "The Lord is my helper; I will not fear. What can man do to me?"

Proverbs 9: 1 - 6 Wisdom has built her house, she has hewn out her seven pillars; she has slaughtered her meat, she has mixed her wine, she has also furnished her table. She has sent out her maidens, she cries out from the highest places of the city, "Whoever is simple, let him turn in here!" As for him who lacks understanding, she says to him, "Come, eat of my bread and drink of the wine I have mixed. Forsake foolishness and live, and go in the way of understanding."

Your take:

78. Wash your hands frequently; it's just plain good for your health.

Job 17:9 Yet the righteous will hold to his way, and he who has clean hands will be stronger and stronger.

Matthew 27: 24 – 25 When Pilate saw that he could not prevail at all, but rather that a tumult was rising, he took water and washed his hands before the multitude, saying, "I am innocent of the blood of this just person. You see to it. And then all the people answered and said, "His blood be on us and on our children."

Your take:

79. Life gets easier if you realize others around you are not perfect either.

Hebrews 12:14 Pursue peace with all people, and holiness, without which no one will see the Lord: looking carefully lest anyone fall short of the grace of God; lest any root of bitterness springing up cause trouble, and by this many become defiled; lest there be any fornicator or profane person like Esau, who for one morsel of food sold his birthright.

Your take:

80. Learn from your mistakes and you gain something, even in your loss.

Genesis 45: 4 – 6 And Joseph said to his brothers, "Please come near to me." So they came near. Then he said: "I am Joseph your brother, whom you sold into Egypt. But now, do not therefore be grieved or angry with yourselves because you sold me here; for God sent me before you to preserve life. For these two years the famine has been in the land, and there are still five years in which there will be neither plowing nor harvesting."

Genesis 45:28 Then Israel said, "It is enough. Joseph my son is still alive. I will go and see him before I die."

Genesis 46: 2 – 4 Then God spoke to Israel in visions in the night, and said, "Jacob, Jacob!" And he said, "Here I am." So He said, I am God, the God of your father; do not fear to go down to Egypt, for I will make of you a great nation there. I will go down with you to Egypt, and I will also surely bring you up again; and Joseph will put his hand on your eyes."

Your take:

81. Prayer does what no other act can do, it moves the hand of God.

Numbers 21: 7 - 8 Therefore the people came to Moses, and said, "We have sinned, for we have spoken against the Lord and against you; pray to the Lord that He take away the serpents from us." Then the Lord said to Moses, "Make a fiery serpent, and set it on a pole; and it shall be that everyone who is bitten, when he looks at it, shall live."

Your take:

82. When you yell, you encourage others to yell, but a soft response dispels conflict.

1 Thessalonians 2: 10 - 12 You are witnesses, and God also, how devoutly and justly and blamelessly we behaved ourselves among you who believe; as you know how we exhorted and comforted, and charged every one of you, as a father does his own children, that you would walk worthy of God who calls you into His own kingdom and glory.

Your take:

83. Work, because of His love, makes the world go around.

John 5: 15 - 18 The man departed and told the Jews that it was Jesus who had made him well. For this reason the Jews persecuted Jesus, and sought to kill him, because He had done these things on the Sabbath. But Jesus answered them, "My Father has been working until now, and I have been working." Therefore the Jews sought all the more to kill Him, because He not only broke the Sabbath, but also said that God was His Father, making Himself equal with God.

Your take:

84. Words (good news) are just plain good preventative medicine.

Romans 1: 16 – 17 For I am not ashamed of the gospel of Christ, for it is the power of God to salvation for everyone who believes, for Jew first and also for the Greek. For in it the righteousness of God is revealed from faith to faith; as it is written, "The just shall live by faith."

Hebrews 7: 23 – 25 Also there were many priests, because they were prevented by death from continuing. But He, because He continues forever, has an unchangeable priesthood. Therefore He is also able to save to the uttermost those who come to God through Him, since He always lives to make intercession for them.

Your take:

85. Make a list, you will probably accomplish more and save wasted steps.

Psalm 20: 4 - 5 May He grant you according to your heart's desire, and fulfill all your purpose. We will rejoice in your salvation, and in the name of our God we will set up our banners! May the Lord fulfill all your petitions.

2 Corinthians 1: 17 - 20 Therefore, when I was planning this, did I do it lightly? Or the things I plan, do I plan according to the flesh, that with me there should be yes, yes, and no, no? But as God is faithful, our word to you was not yes and no. For the Son of God, Jesus Christ, who was preached among you by us- by me, Silvanus, and Timothy, was not

yes and no, but in Him was yes. For all the promises of God in Him are yes, and in Him Amen, to the glory of God through us.

Your take:

86. A few extra minutes of planning may save hours of time.

Luke 12: 33 - 34 Sell what you have and give alms; provide yourselves money bags which do not grow old, a treasure in the heavens that does not fail, where no thief approaches nor moth destroys. For where your treasure is, there your heart will be also.

Luke 12: 43 - 44 Blessed is that servant whom his master will find so doing when he comes. Truly, I say to you that he will make him ruler over all that he has.

Your take:

87. When no one else but you knows, God knows.

1 Samuel 2:3 Talk no more so very proudly; let no arrogance come from your mouth, for the Lord is the God of knowledge; and by Him actions are weighed.

Luke 1: 50 - 52 And His mercy is on those who fear Him from generation to generation. He has shown strength with His arm; He has scattered the proud in the imagination of their hearts. He has put down the mighty from their thrones, and exalted the lowly.

Your take:

88. Pursuit peace, not war.

Isaiah 32: 16 – 17 Then justice will dwell in the wilderness, and righteousness remain in the fruitful field. The work of righteousness will be peace, and the effect of righteousness, quietness and assurance forever.

Psalm 34: 14 – 16 Depart from evil and do good; seek peace and pursue it. The eyes of the Lord are on the righteous, and His ears are open to their cry. The face of the Lord is against those who do evil, to cut off the remembrance of them from the earth.

Your take:

89. A house is built one day at a time, so it is with a friendship.

Psalm 122: 6 – 9 Pray for the peace of Jerusalem: "May they prosper who love you. Peace be within your walls, prosperity within your palaces." For the sake of my brethren and companions, I will now say, "Peace be within you." Because of the house of the Lord our God I will seek your good.

Your take:

90. Strive to learn something new each day.

Psalm 119: 73 – 74 Your hands have made me and fashioned me; Give me understanding, that I may learn Your commandments. Those who fear You will be glad when they see me, because I have hoped in Your word.

John 15: 15 – 16 No longer do I call you servants, for a servant does not know what his master is doing; but I have called you friends, for all things that I heard from My Father I have made known to you. You did not choose Me, but I chose you and appointed you that you should go and bear fruit, and that your fruit remain, that whatever you ask the Father in My name He may give you.

Your take:

91. Engage only in battles where there is at least some chance of a good outcome.

Numbers 10:9 When you go to war in your land against the enemy who oppresses you, then you shall sound an alarm with the trumpets, and you will be remembered before the Lord your God, and you will be saved from your enemies.

Jeremiah 49:2 "Therefore behold, the days are coming," says the Lord, "That I will cause to be heard an alarm of war in Rabbah of the Ammonites; it shall be a desolate mound, and her villages shall be burned with fire. Then Israel shall take possession of his inheritance," says the Lord.

Your take:

92. Give respect and courteousness where it is due.
Leviticus 19: 1 – 3 And the Lord spoke to Moses, saying, "Speak to all the congregation of the children of Israel, and say to them: you shall be holy, for I the Lord your God am holy. Every one of you shall revere his mother and father, and keep My Sabbaths: I am the Lord you God."

Your take:


93. Keep order in your closet to help you find what you need when you need it.
1 Thessalonians 2: 9 – 12 For you remember, brethren, our labor and toil; for laboring night and day, that we might not be a burden to any of you, we preached to you the gospel of God. You are witnesses, and God also, how devoutly and justly and blamelessly we behaved ourselves among you who believe; as you know how we exhorted, and comforted , and charged every one of you, as a father does his own children, that you would walk worthy of God who calls you into His own kingdom and glory.

Your take:

94. Don't let anyone, or anything take your joy away. Your joy comes from the Lord.
Psalm 5: 11 – 12 But let all those rejoice who put their trust in You; let them ever shout for joy, because You defend them; let those also who love Your name be joyful in You. For You, O Lord, will bless the righteous; with favor. You will surround him as with a shield.

John 16:22 Therefore you now have sorrow; but I will see you again and your heart will rejoice, and your joy no one will take away from you.

Your take:


95. Show honor to others, it will reassure you of their value, and also help them to see their own self-worth.

Exodus 20:12 "Honor your father and mother, that your days may be long upon the land which the Lord your God is giving you."

James 2: 8 – 9 If you really fulfill the royal law according to the Scripture, "You shall love your neighbor as yourself," you do well; but if you show partiality, you commit sin, and are convicted by the law as transgressors.

Your take:

96. Over scheduling is like trying to pack too much into your suitcase.

Exodus 1: 11- 13 Therefore they set taskmasters over them to afflict them with their burdens. And they built for Pharaoh supply cities, Pithom and Raamses. But the more they afflicted them, the more they multiplied and grew. And they were in dread of the children of Israel. So the Egyptians made the children of Israel serve with rigor.

Ecclesiastes 2: 23 – 24 For all his days are sorrowful, and his work burdensome; even in the night his heart takes no rest. This also is vanity. Nothing is better for a man than that he should eat and drink, and that his soul should enjoy good in his labor. This also, I saw, was from the hand of God.

Your take:

97. One car running gets you further than several broken.

Psalm 89: 40 - 41 You have broken down all his hedges; You have brought his strongholds to ruin. All who pass the way plunder him; He is a reproach to his neighbors.

Your take:

98. Eat when you're hungry, stop when you are full.

Proverbs 23: 1 – 3 When you sit down to eat with a ruler, consider carefully what is before you; and put a knife to your throat if you are a man given to appetite. Do not desire his delicacies, for they are deceptive food.

Your take:

99. Everyone has a love language, look for the right one for those you care for.

Esther 4:16 "Go, gather all the Jews who are present in Shushan, and fast for me; neither eat nor drink for three days, night or day. My maids and I will fast likewise. And so I will go to the king, which is against the law; and if I perish, I perish!"

Proverbs 3:11 My son, do not despise the chastening of the Lord, nor detest His correction; for whom the Lord loves He corrects, just as a father the son in whom he delights.

Your take:

100. The difference between a window and a mirror. One looks forward while the other looks backward.

James 1: 23 – 25 For if anyone is a hearer of the word and not a doer, he is like a man observing his natural face in a mirror; for he observes himself, goes away, and immediately forgets what kind of man he was. But he who looks into the perfect law of liberty and continues in it, and is not a forgetful hearer but a doer of the work, this one will be blessed in what he does.

2 Corinthians 3:18 But we all, with unveiled face, beholding as in a mirror the glory of the Lord, are being transformed into the same image from glory to glory, just as by the Spirit of the Lord.

Your take:

101. Opening a door reveals what is on the other side.

Matthew 7: 7 - 9 Ask, and it will be given to you; seek and you will find; knock, and it will be opened to you. For everyone who asks receives, and he who seeks finds, and to him who knock it will be opened. Or what man is there among you who, if his son asks for bread, will give him a stone?

Colossians 4:2 Continue earnestly in prayer, being vigilant in it with thanksgiving; meanwhile praying also for us, that God would open to us a door for the word, to speak the mystery of Christ, for which I am also in chains, that I may make it manifest, as I ought to speak.

Your take:

102. The invention of the wheel changed how most of us get about.

1 Kings 7: 32 – 33 Under the panels were the four wheels, and the axles of the wheels were joined to the cart. The height of a wheel was one and a half cubits. The workmanship of the wheels was like the workmanship of a chariot wheel; their axle pins, their rims, their spokes, and their hubs were all of cast bronze.

Your take:

103. One picture tells only a small questionable part of the whole story.

Matthew 28: 11: - 14 Now while they were going, behold some of the guard came into the city and reported to the chief priests all the things that had happened. When they had assembled with the elders and consulted together, they gave a large sum of money to the soldiers, saying, "Tell them, 'His disciples came at night and stole Him away while we slept. And if this comes to the governor's ears, we will appease him and make you secure." So they took the money and did as they were instructed; and this saying is commonly reported among the Jews until this day.

Your take:

104. Yes or no can be the right answer depending upon the question and circumstances.

Luke 20: 3 - 8 But He answered and said to them, "I also will ask you one thing, and answer Me; The baptism of John – was it from heaven or from men?" And they reasoned among themselves, saying, "If we say, 'From heaven,' He will say, "Why then did you not believe him?" But if we say, 'From men,' all the people will stone us, for they are persuaded that John was a prophet." So they answered that they did not know where it was from. And Jesus said to them, "Neither will I tell you by what authority I do these things."

Your take:

105. The sandal, the horse, the cart and the auto are each measurements of time passed.

Isaiah 49: 8 – 9 Thus says the Lord: "In an acceptable time I have heard You, and in the day of salvation I have helped You; I will preserve You and give You as a covenant to the people, to restore the earth, to cause them to inherit the desolate heritages; that You may say to the prisoners, 'Go forth,' to those who are in darkness, 'Show yourselves.'

Luke 6: 37 – 38 "Judge not, and you shall not be judged. Condemn not, and you shall not be condemned. Forgive, and you will be forgiven. Give, and it will be given to you: good measure, pressed down, shaken together, and running over will be put into your bosom. For with the same measure that you use, it will be measured back to you."

Your take:

106. A book gathering dust on a shelf give only a slight glimpse of the possible treasures inside.

2 King 23: 2 – 3 The king went up to the house of the Lord with all the men of Judah, and with him all the inhabitants of Jerusalem – the priests and the prophets and all the people, both small and great. And he read in their hearing all the words of the Book of the covenant which had been found in the house of the Lord. Then the king stood

by a pillar and made a covenant before the Lord, to follow the Lord and to keep His commandments and His testimonies and His statutes, with all his heart and all his soul, to perform the words of this covenant that were written in this book. And all the people took a stand for the covenant.

Your take:

107. God told us that obedience is better than sacrifice.

1 Samuel 15: 22 – 23 So Samuel said: "Has the Lord as great delight in burnt offerings and sacrifices, as in obeying the voice of the Lord? Behold, to obey is better than sacrifice, and to heed than the fat of rams. For rebellion is as the sin of witchcraft, and stubbornness is as iniquity and idolatry. Because you have rejected the word of the Lord, He also has rejected you from being king."

Your take:

108. Be careful what you ask for, you may get it, and then cry out because it isn't what you expected it to be.

Isaiah 8: 5 – 7 The Lord also spoke to me again, saying: "Inasmuch as these people refused the waters of Shiloah that flow softly, and rejoice in Rezin and in Remaliah's son; now therefore, behold, the Lord brings up over them the waters of the River, strong and mighty – the king of Assyria and all his glory; he will go up over all his channels and go over all his banks.

Your Take:

109. God's Word is final and complete, it's all we need to have the truth.

Psalm 18: 30 – 32 As for God, His way is perfect; the word of the Lord is proven; He is a shield to all who trust in Him. For who is God, except the Lord? And who is a rock, except our God?" It is God who arms me with strength, and makes my way perfect.

John 8:51 "Most assuredly, I say to you, if anyone keeps My word he shall never see death."
Your take:

110. When you fail to plan, you plan to fail.
Psalm 89: 31 – 33 "If they break My statutes and do not keep My commandments, then I will punish their transgression with the rod, and their iniquity with stripes. Nevertheless, My lovingkindness I will not utterly take from him, nor allow My faithfulness to fail."
Proverbs 15:22 Without counsel, plans go awry, but in the multitude of counselors they are established.
Your take:

111. A man's good integrity has greater value than his wealth.
Psalm 78: 70 – 72 He also chose David His servant, and took him from the sheepfolds; from following the ewes that had young He brought him to shepherd Jacob His people, and Israel His inheritance. So he shepherded them according to the integrity of his heart, and guided them by the skillfulness of his hands.
1 Kings 9: 4 – 5 "Now if you walk before Me as your father David walked, in integrity of heart and in uprightness, to do according to all that I have commanded you, and if you keep My statutes and My judgments, then I will establish the throne of your kingdom over Israel forever, as I promised David your father, saying, you shall not fail to have a man on the throne of Israel."
Your take:

112. A man's toys are fun, but can be problems for him as well.
Psalm 24: 4 – 5 He who has clean hands and a pure heart, who has not lifted up his soul to an idol, nor sworn deceitfully. He shall receive blessing from the Lord, and righteousness from the God of his salvation.

1 Corinthians 8:1 – 3 Now concerning things offered to idols; We know that we all have knowledge. Knowledge puffs up, but love edifies. And if anyone thinks that he knows anything, he knows nothing yet as he ought to know. But if anyone loves God, this one is known by Him.
Your take:

113. A loan given becomes a gift only when there is no repayment plan.
Proverbs 18:16 A man's gift makes room for him, and brings him before great men.
Luke 11: 13 "If you then, being evil, know how to give good gifts to your children, how much more will your heavenly father give the Holy Spirit to those who ask Him!"
Your take:

114. Time is precious, you only get so much of it.
Matthew 28: 18 – 20 And Jesus came and spoke to them, saying, "All authority has been given to Me in heaven and on earth. Go therefore and make disciples of all the nations, baptizing them in the name of the Father and of the Son and of the Holy Spirit, teaching them to observe all things that I have commanded you; and lo, I am with you always, even to the end of the age." Amen
Luke 24: 44 – 45 Then He said to them, "These are the words which I spoke to you while I was still with you, that all things must be fulfilled which were written in the law of Moses and the Prophets and the Psalms concerning Me." And He opened their understanding, that they might comprehend the Scriptures.
Your take:

115. Be courteous to others even when they don't reciprocate.
Numbers 14:18 – 19 The Lord is longsuffering and abundant in mercy, forgiving iniquity and transgression; but He by no means clears the guilty, visiting the iniquity of the fathers on the children to the

third and fourth generation. Pardon the iniquity of this people, I pray, according to the greatness of Your mercy, just as You have forgiven this people, from Egypt even until now.

Matthew 5: 44 – 46 But I say to you, love your enemies, bless those who curse you, do good to those who hate you, and pray for those who spitefully use you and persecute you, that you may be sons of your Father in heaven; for He makes His sun rise on the evil and on the good, and send rain on the just and the unjust. For if you love those who love you, what reward have you? Do not even the tax collectors do the same?

Your take:

116. Truth, integrity and compassion make for a wonderful recipe.

Titus 2: 11 – 14 For the grace of God that brings salvation has appeared to all men, teaching us that, denying ungodliness and worldly lust, we should love soberly, righteously, and godly in the present age, looking for the blessed hope and glorious appearing of our great God and Savior Jesus Christ, who gave Himself for us, that He might redeem us from every lawless deed and purify for Himself His own special people, zealous for good works.

Proverbs 10: 8 – 9 The wise in heart will receive commands, but a prating fool will fall. He who walks with integrity walks securely, but he who perverts his ways will become known.

Romans 9: 15 -16 For He says to Moses, "I will have mercy on whomever I will have mercy, and I will have compassion on whomever I will have compassion. So then it is not of him who wills, nor of him who runs, but of God who shows mercy.

Your take:

117. When nothing in this world satisfies you, remember your Creator has another PLACE in mind for you.

Matthew 24: 43 – 44 But know this, that if the master of the house had known what hour the thief would come, he would have watched and not allowed his house to be broken into. Therefore you also be ready, for the Son of Man is coming at an hour you do not expect.

Luke 21: 27 – 28 Then they will see the Son of Man coming in a cloud with power and great glory. Now when these things begin to happen, look up and lift up your heads, because your redemption draws near.

Your take:

118. Hug several trees today, they do so much for us.

Genesis 2: 16 – 17 And Lord God commanded the man, saying, "Of every tree of the garden you may freely eat, but of the tree of the knowledge of good and evil you shall not eat, for in the day that you eat of it you shall surely die."

Luke 21: 29 – 30 Then He spoke to them a parable: look at the fig tree, and all the trees. When they are already budding, you see and know for yourselves that summer is now near.

Your take:

119. April 15th is tax deadline every year, except in 2020. It's was in July.

Matthew 17:24 -25 When they had come to Capernaum, those who received the temple tax came to Peter and said, "Does your Teacher not pay the temple tax?" He said, "Yes." And when he had come into the house, Jesus anticipated him, saying, "What do you think, Simon? From whom do the kings of the earth take customs and taxes, from their sons or from strangers?"

Your take:

120. A good neighborhood idea is to have a "share a book, corner box."

Isaiah 58:10 If you extend your soul to the hungry and satisfy the afflicted soul, then your light shall dawn in the darkness, and your darkness shall be as the noonday.

Ephesians 4:28 Let him who stole steal no longer, but rather let him labor, working with his hands what is good, that he may have something to give him who has a need.

Your take:


121. What percentage of what you hear and read today is true? Only God's Word is 100%.

Isaiah 40:8 The grass withers, the flower fades, but the word of our God stands forever.

John 17:17 – 20 Sanctify them by Your truth. Your word is truth. As You sent Me into the world, I also have sent them into the world. And for their sakes I sanctify Myself, that they also may be sanctified by the truth.

Your take:


122. What really makes for contentment? Answer = Peace of mind.

Numbers 25: 12 – 13 Therefore say, "Behold, I give to him My covenant of peace; and it shall be to him and his descendants after him a covenant of an everlasting priesthood, because he was zealous for his God, and made atonement for the children of Israel."

Isaiah 26:3 You will keep him in perfect peace, whose mind is stayed on You, because he trusts in You.

Your take:


123. Use correct punctuation in your writing to avoid possible misinterpretation.

Psalm 81: 7 – 8 You called in trouble, and I delivered you; I answered you in the secret place of thunder; I tested you at the waters of Meribah. Selah. Hear, O My people, and I will admonish you! O Israel, if you will listen to Me!

Luke 2: 49 – 50 And He said to them, "Why did you seek me? Did you not know that I must be about My Father's business?" But they did not understand the statement which He spoke to them.

Your take:


124. It's best to share your deepest secrets only with your pets, or better yet with the Lord.

Proverbs 16: 27 – 28 An ungodly man digs up evil, and it is on his lips like a burning fire. A perverse man sows strife, and a whisperer separates the best of friends.

1 Timothy 5:13 And besides they learn to be idle, wandering about from house to house, and not only idle but also gossips and busybodies, saying things which they ought not.

Your take:


125. The longer one lives the earlier we look for our pillow.

Proverbs 4:1 - 5 Hear, my children, the instruction of a father, and give attention to know understanding; for I give you good doctrine: do not forsake my law. When I was my father's son, tender and the only one in the sight of my mother, he taught me, and said to me: Let your heart retain my words; keep my commandments, and live. Get wisdom! Get understanding! Do not forget, nor turn away from the words of my mouth.

Your take:


126. There is power in the words we use, speak them wisely.

2 Chronicles 1: 11 - 12 Then God said to Solomon: "Because this was in your heart, and you have not asked riches or wealth or honor or the life of your enemies, nor have you asked long life – but have asked wisdom and knowledge for yourself, that you may judge My people over whom I have made you king – wisdom and knowledge are granted to you; and I will give you riches and wealth and honor, such as none of the kings have had who were before you, nor shall any after you have the like."

Romans 11: 33 – 36 Oh, the depth of the riches both of the wisdom and knowledge of God! How unsearchable are His judgements and His ways past finding out! "For who has known the mind of the Lord? Or who has become His counselor? Or who has first given to Him and it shall be repaid to him?" For of Him and through Him and to Him are all things, to whom be glory forever. Amen

Your take:


127. Your stress level is based upon your reaction level.

Jeremiah 19:15 Thus says the Lord of hosts, the God of Israel; "Behold, I will bring on this city and on all her towns all the doom that I have pronounced against it, because they have stiffened their necks that they might not hear My words."

Your take:


128. An easy chair, a cup of tea and a good book are the makings for a peaceful time.

2 Samuel 9:7 So David said to him, "Do not fear, for I will surely show you kindness for Jonathan your father's sake, and will restore to you all the land of Saul your grandfather; and you shall eat bread at my table continually."

Your take:

129. One picture speaks louder and clearer than one thousand words.

Genesis 31: 51 – 52 Then Laban said to Jacob, "Here is this heap and here is this pillar, which I have placed between you and me. This heap is a witness, and this pillar is a witness, that I will not pass beyond this heap to you and you will not pass beyond this pillar to me, for harm."

Your take:

130. Look for good in every person, it is there, but harder to find in some.

1 Samuel 22: 22 – 23 So David said to Abiathar, "I knew that day, when Doeg the Edomite was there, that he would surely tell Saul. I have caused the death of all the persons of your father's house. Stay with me; do not fear. For he who seeks my life seeks your life, but with me you shall be safe."

Romans 10: 20 – 21 But Isaiah is very bold and says: "I was found by those who did not seek me; I was made manifest to those who did not ask for me." But to Israel he says: "All the day long I have stretched out My hands to a disobedient and contrary people."

Your take:

131. A little comma correctly placed can make a big difference.

Acts 19:32 Some therefore cried one thing and some another, for the assembly was confused, and most of them did not know why they had come together.

Galatians 5: 8 – 10 This persuasion does not come from Him who calls you. A little leaven leavens the whole lump. I have confidence in you, in the Lord, that you will have no other mind; but he who troubles you shall bear his judgment, whoever he is.

Your take:


132. Life is short, so do the important things first.

Exodus 2: 2 – 4 So the woman conceived and bore a son. And when she saw that he was a beautiful child, she hid him three months. But when she could no longer hide him, she took an ark of bulrushes for him, daubed it with asphalt and pitch, put the child in it, and laid it in the reeds by the river bank. And his sister stood afar off, to know what would be done to him.

Isaiah 29: 17 – 19 Is it not yet a very little while till Lebanon shall be turned into a fruitful field, and the fruitful field be esteemed as a forest? In that day the deaf shall hear the words of the book, and the eyes of the blind shall see out of obscurity and out of darkness. The humble also shall increase their joy in the Lord, and the poor among men shall rejoice in the Holy One of Israel.

Your take:


133. God knows, if you knew when your life was over, would it make a difference?

Isaiah 30: 18 – 19 Therefore the Lord will wait, that He may be gracious to you; and therefore He will be exalted, that He may have mercy on you. For the Lord is a God of justice; blessed are all those who wait for Him. For the people shall dwell in Zion at Jerusalem; you shall weep no more. He will be very gracious to you at the sound of your cry; when He hears it, He will answer you.

Mark 13: 19 – 20 For in those days there will be tribulation, such as has not been since the beginning of the creation which God created until this time, nor ever shall be. And unless the Lord had shortened those days, no flesh would be saved; but for the elect's sake, whom He chose, He shortened the days.

Your take:


134. The tongue can either build up or it can tear down.

Job 31: 13 – 14 If I have despised the cause of my male and female servant when they complained against me, what then shall I do when God rises up? When He punishes, how shall I answer him?

James 3: 8 – 10 But no man can tame the tongue. It is an unruly evil, full of deadly poison. With it we bless our God and Father, and with it we curse men, who have been made in the similitude of God. Out of the same mouth proceed blessing and cursing. My brethren, these things ought not to be so.

Your take:


135. What is your preference a barrier or a bridge?

Ephesians 2: 14 – 15 For He Himself is our peace, who has made both one, and has broken down the middle wall of separation, having abolished in His flesh the enmity, that is, the law of commandments contained in ordinances, so as to create in Himself one new man from the two, thus making peace, and that He might reconcile them both to God in one body through the cross, thereby putting to death the enmity.

Proverbs 2: 20 - 22 So you may walk in the way of goodness, and keep to the paths of righteousness. For the upright will dwell in the land, and the blameless will remain in it; but the wicked will be cut off from the earth; and the unfaithful will be uprooted from it.

Your take:

136. Most every day we hear old words being used in new ways.

Psalm 19: 1 – 4 The heavens declare the glory of God; and the firmament show His handiwork. Day unto day utters speech, and night unto night reveals knowledge. There is no speech nor language where their voice is not heard. Their line has gone out through all the earth, and their words to the end of the world.

1 Corinthians 14: 10 – 12 There are, it may be, so many kinds of languages in the world, and none of them is without significance. Therefore, if I do not know the meaning of the language, I shall be a foreigner to him who speaks, and he who speaks will be a foreigner to me. Even so you, since you are zealous for spiritual gifts, let it be for the edification of the church that you seek to excel.

Your take:

137. It is better to keep your mouth shut than stick your foot in it.

Proverbs 18: 6 – 7 A fool's lips enter into contention, and his mouth calls for blows. A fool's mouth is his destruction, and his lips are the snare of his soul.

Matthew 7: 26 – 27 "But everyone who hears these sayings of Mine, and does not do them, will be like a foolish man who built his house on the sand: and the rain descended, the floods came, and the wind blew and beat on that house; and it fell. And great was its fall."

Your take:

138. God knows and you know, and that all that's important at the end of your days.

Ezekiel 24:14 "I, the Lord, have spoken it; It shall come to pass, and I will do it; I will not hold back, nor will I spare, nor will I relent; according to your ways and according to your deeds they will judge you," says the Lord God.

Hossa 12:2 The Lord also brings a charge against Judah, and will punish Jacob according to his way; according to his deeds He will recompense him.
Your take:


139. When we finally show up in His Court He already knows all that we did.
Zechariah 3:7 "Thus says the Lord of hosts: 'If you will walk in My ways, and if you will keep My command, then you shall also judge My house, and likewise have charge of My courts; I will give you places to walk among these who stand here.'
John 7: 16 – 17 Jesus answered them and said, "My doctrine is not Mine, but His who sent Me. If anyone wills to do His will, he shall know concerning the doctrine, whether it is from God or whether I speak on My own authority.
Your take:


140. A paper can have both good news and bad news on the same page.
Psalm 112: 7 – 8 He will not be afraid of evil tidings; His heart is steadfast, trusting in the Lord. His heart is established; he will not be afraid, until he sees his desire upon his enemies.
Acts 13: 33 – 34 God has fulfilled this for us their children, in that He has raised up Jesus. As it is written in the second Psalm; "You are My Son, today I have begotten you." And that He raised Him from the dead, no more to return to corruption, He has spoken thus: "I will give you the sure mercies of David."
Your take:


141. Properly following instruction can make a big difference.

Ezra 10: 7 – 8 And they issued a proclamation throughout Judah and Jerusalem to all the descendants of the captivity, that they must gather at Jerusalem, and that whoever would not come within three days, according to the instructions of the leaders and elders, all his property would be confiscated, and he himself would be separated from the assembly of those from the captivity.

Acts 5: 41 – 42 So they departed from the presence of the council, rejoicing that they were counted worthy to suffer shame for His name. And daily in the temple, and in every house, they did not cease teaching and preaching Jesus as the Christ.

Your take:


142. To some, everyday feels like Monday, but to others, everyday feels like Friday.

Matthew 20: 11 – 15 And when they had received it, they complained against the landlord, saying, 'These last men have worked only one hour, and you made them equal to us who have borne the burden and the heat of the day.' But he answered one of them and said, 'Friend, I am doing you no wrong. Did you not agree with me for a denarius? Take what is yours and go your way. I wish to give to this last man the same as to you. Is it not lawful for me to do what I wish with my own things?'

Your take:


143. Let your joy be known to all around you.

Psalm 5: 11 -12 But let those rejoice who put their trust in You; let them ever shout for joy, because You defend them; let those who love Your name be joyful in You. For You, O Lord, will bless the righteous; with favor You will surround him as with a shield.

Your take:

144. Some live like a microwave while some others live like a slow cooker. Who are all the TWEENERS?

1 Corinthians 11: 19 – 22 For there must also be factions among you, that those who are approved may be recognized among you. Therefore when you come together in one place, it is not to eat the Lord's Supper. For in eating, each one takes his own supper ahead of others; and one is hungry and another is drunk.

Your take:


145. God's word tells us we are fearfully and wonderfully made, and also that no two of us are exactly alike.

Psalm 139: 14 – 18 I will praise You, for I am fearfully and wonderfully made; marvelous are Your works, and that my soul knows very well. My frame was not hidden from You, when I was made in secret, and skillfully wrought in the lowest parts of the earth. Your eyes saw my substance, being yet formed. And in Your book they all were written, the days fashioned for me, when as yet there were none of them. How precious also are your thoughts to me, O God! How great is the sum of them! If I should count them, they would be more in number than the sand; when I awake, I am still with You.

Your take:


146. Good news is coming for those willing to wait.

Isaiah 40: 30 – 31 Even the youths shall faint and be weary, and the young men shall utterly fall, but those who wait on the Lord shall renew their strength; they shall mount up with wings like eagles, they shall run and not be weary, they shall walk and not faint.

Psalm 27:14 Wait on the Lord; be of good courage, and He shall strengthen your heart; wait, I say, on the Lord.

Proverbs 20:22 Do not say, "I will recompense evil"; Wait for the Lord, and He will save you.

Your take:


147. The ONLY difference between "<u>Good and God</u>" is the extra letter (o.)

Genesis 1:31 Then God saw everything that He had made, and indeed it was very good. So the evening and the morning were the sixth day.

Psalm 106:1 Praise the Lord! Oh give thanks to the Lord, for He is good! For His mercy endures forever.

Your take:


148. Listen to good advice with both ears.

Psalm 78: 1 – 4 Give ear, O my people, to my Law; incline your ears to the words of my mouth. I will open my mouth in a parable. I will utter dark sayings of old, which we have heard and known, and our fathers have told us. We will not hide them from their children, telling to the generation to come the praises of the Lord, and His strength and His wonderful works that He has done.

John 10: 3 – 5 To him the doorkeeper opens, and the sheep hear his voice; and he calls his own sheep by name and leads them out. And when he brings out his own sheep, he goes before them; and the sheep follow him, for they know his voice. Yet they will by no means follow a stranger, but will flee from him, for they do not know the voice of strangers.

Your take:

149. Always speak the truth, but with love.

Ephesians 4: 11 – 16 And He Himself gave some to be apostles, some prophets, some evangelists, and some pastors and teachers, for the equipping of the saints for the work of the ministry, for the edifying of the body of Christ, till we all come to the unity of the faith and of the knowledge of the Son of God, to a perfect man, to the measure of the stature of the fullness of Christ, that we should no longer be children, tossed to and fro and carried about with every wind of doctrine, by the trickery of men, in the cunning craftiness of deceitful plotting, but speaking the truth in love, may grow up in all things into Him who is the head – Christ – from whom the whole body, joined and knit together by what every joint supplies, according to the effective working by which every part does its share, causes growth of the body for the deifying of itself in love.

Your take:


150. Not everything should be put in a box.

2 Chronicles 7: 13 – 16 When I shut up heaven and there is no rain, or command the locusts to devour the land, or send pestilence among My people, if My people who are called by My name will humble themselves, and pray and seek My face, and turn from their wicked ways, then I will hear from heaven, and will forgive their sin and heal their land. Now My eyes will be open and My ears attentive to prayer made in this place. For now I have chosen and sanctified this house, that My name may be there forever; and My eyes and My heart will be there perpetually.

Psalm 119: 65 – 66 You have dealt well with your servant, O Lord, according to Your word. Teach me good judgement and knowledge, for I believe Your commandments.

Your take:

151. Road signs are very important in most any journey.

Exodus 14: 15 – 17 And the Lord said to Moses, "Why do you cry to Me? Tell the children of Israel to go forward. But lift up your rod, and stretch out your hand over the sea and divide it. And the children of Israel shall go on dry ground through the midst of the sea. And I indeed will harden the hearts of the Egyptians, and they shall follow them. So I will gain honor over Pharaoh and over all his army, his chariots, and his horsemen.

Mark 13: 4 – 6 "Tell us, when will these things be? And what will be the sign when all these things will be fulfilled?" And Jesus, answering them, began to say, "Take heed that no one deceives you. For many will come in My name, saying 'I am He,' and will deceive many. But when you hear of wars and rumors of wars, do not be troubled; for such things must happen, but the end is not yet."

Your take:


152. Most people appreciate it when others show up on time.

Luke 21: 25 – 28 "And there will be signs in the sun, and the moon, and in the stars; and on the earth distress of nations, with perplexity, the sea and the waves roaring; men's hearts failing them from fear and the expectation of those things which are coming on the earth, for the powers of the heavens will be shaken. Then they will see the Son of Man coming in a cloud with power and great glory. Now when these things begin to happen, look up and lift up your heads, because your redemption draws near."

Revelation 3:3 Remember therefore how you have received and heard; hold fast and repent. Therefore if you will not watch, I will come upon you as a thief, and you will not know what hour I will come upon you.

Your take:

153. A drawer is to conceal while a shelf is to display.

Proverbs 21:14 A gift in secret pacifies anger, and a bribe behind the back strong wrath.

Luke 2: 25 – 29 And behold, there was a man in Jerusalem whose name was Simeon, and this man was just and devout, waiting for the Consolation of Israel, and the Holy Spirit was upon him. And it had been revealed to him by the Holy Spirit that he would not see death before he had seen the Lord's Christ. So he came by the Spirit into the temple. And when the parents brought in the Child Jesus, to do for Him according to the custom of the law, he took Him up in his arms and blessed God and said, "Lord, now You are letting Your servant depart in peace, according to Your word; for my eyes have seen Your salvation which You have prepared before the face of all peoples, a light to bring revelation to the Gentiles, and the glory of Your people Israel."

Your take:


154. Red is to stop, yellow is to use caution and green is to go.

1 Samuel 23: 1 – 2 Then they told David, saying, "Look, the Philistines are fighting against Keilah, and they are robbing the threshing floors." Therefore David inquired of the Lord, saying, "Shall I go and attack these Philistines?" And the Lord said to David, "Go and attack the Philistines, and save Keilah."

1 Samuel 26: 10 – 11 David said furthermore, "As the Lord lives, the Lord shall strike him, or his day shall come to die, or he shall go out to battle and perish. The Lord forbid that I should stretch out my hand against the Lord's anointed. But please, take now the spear and the jug of water that are by Saul's head, and let us go."

Your take:

155. A smooth route is good to ride on.

Deuteronomy 2: 27 – 28 Let me pass through your land; I will keep strictly to the road, and I will turn neither to the right nor to the left. You shall sell me food for money, that I may eat, and give me water for money, that I may drink; only let me pass through on foot.

Matthew 21: 8 – 9 And a very great multitude spread their clothes on the road; others cut branches from the trees and spread them on the road. Then the multitudes who went before and those who followed cried out, saying: "Hosanna to the Son of David! Blessed is He who comes in the name of the Lord! Hosanna in the highest!"

Your take:


156. Finding your way on a dark night requires proper lighting.

Psalm 119:105 Your word is a lamp to my feet and a light to my path.

Ecclesiastes 2: 12 – 14 Then I turned myself to consider wisdom and madness and folly; for what can the man do who succeeds the king? – Only what he has already done. Then I saw that wisdom excels folly as light excels darkness. The wise man's eyes are in his head, but the fool walks in darkness. Yet I myself perceived that the same event happens to them all.

Your take:


157. Saving time and money should help your future.

1 Corinthians 16: 1 – 2 Now concerning the collection for the saints, as I have given orders to the churches of Galatia, so you must do also: On the first day of the week let each one of you lay something aside, storing up as he may prosper, that there be no collections when I come.

James 4: 13 – 15 Come now, you who say, "Today or tomorrow we will go to such and such a city, spend a year there, buy and sell, and make a profit"; whereas you do not know what will happen tomorrow. For what is your life? It is even a vapor that appears for a little time and then vanishes away. Instead you ought to say, "If the Lord wills, we shall live and do this or that."

Your take:


158. A body of water is normally easier to cross with a ship or boat.

Joshua 3:1 Then Joshua rose early in the morning; and they set out from Acacia Grove and came to the Jordon, he and all the children of Israel, and lodged there before they crossed over.

Acts 21: 2 - 3 And finding a ship sailing over to Phoenicia, we went aboard and set sail. When we had sighted Cyprus, we passed it on the left, sailed to Syria, and landed at Tyre; for there the ship was to unload her cargo.

Your take:


159. Someone said, "The pen is mightier than the sword."

Genesis 42: 14 – 17 But Joseph said to them, "It is as I spoke to you, saying, 'You are spies!' In this manner you shall be tested: By the life of Pharaoh, you shall not leave this place unless your youngest brother comes here. Send one of you, and let him bring your brother; and you shall be kept in prison, that your words may be tested to see whether there is any truth in you; or else, by the life of Pharaoh, surely you are spies!" So he put them all together in prison three days.

John 3:5 – 6 Jesus answered and said, "Most assuredly, I say to you, unless one is born of water and the Spirit, he cannot enter the kingdom of God. That which is born of the flesh is flesh, and that which is born of the Spirit is spirit. Do not marvel that I said to you, 'You must be born again.' The wind blows where it wishes, and you hear the sound of it, but cannot tell where it comes from and where it goes. So is everyone who is born of the Spirit."

Your take:


160. A kind word spoken can help to win over most differences.

2 Chronicles 10:7 And they spoke to him, saying, "If you are kind to these people, and please them, and speak good words to them, they will be your servants forever."

1 John 3: 18 – 20 My little children, let us not love in word or in tongue, but in deed and in truth. And by this we know that we are of the truth, and shall assure our hearts before Him. For if our heart condemns us, God is greater than our heart, and knows all things. Beloved, if our heart does not condemn us, we have confidence toward God.

Your take:


161. Diplomacy, truth and consideration are vital in any debate.

Matthew 5: 14 – 16 "You are the light of the world. A city that is set on a hill cannot be hidden. Nor do they light a lamp and put it under a basket, but on a lampstand, and it gives light to all who are in the house. Let your light so shine before men, that they may see your good works and glorify your Father in heaven."

Luke 15: 6 – 7 "And when he comes home, he calls together his friends and neighbors, saying to them, 'Rejoice with me, for I have found my sheep which was lost!' I say to you that likewise there will be more joy in heaven over one sinner who repents than over ninety-nine just persons who need no repentance."

Your take:

162. Laughter is much like a good medicine.
Proverbs 17:22 A merry heart does good, like a medicine.
Proverbs 17:27 He who has knowledge spares his words, and a man of understanding is of a calm spirit.
Your take:


163. God told us to build our house on solid ground, not on the sand.
Deuteronomy 8: 11 – 12 Beware that you do not forget the Lord your God by not keeping His commandments, His judgements, and His statutes which I command you today, lest – when you have eaten and are full, and have built beautiful houses and dwell in them; and when your herds and your flocks multiply, and your silver and your gold are multiplied, and all that you have is multiplied; when your heart is lifted up, and you forget the Lord your God who brought you out of the Land of Egypt, from the house of bondage, who led you through the great and terrible wilderness, in which were fiery serpents and scorpions and thirsty land where there was no water; who brought water to you out of the flinty rock; who fed you in the wilderness with manna, which your fathers did not know, that He might humble you and that He might test you, to do you good in the end – then you say in your heart, 'My power and the might of my hand have gained me this wealth.'
Proverbs 24: 3 – 4 Through wisdom a house is build, and by understanding it is established; by knowledge the rooms are filled with all precious and pleasant riches.
Your take:


164. One deceptive statement often requires another.

Colossian 2:8 - 10 Beware lest anyone cheat you through philosophy and empty deceit, according to the tradition of men, according to the basic principles of the world, and not according to Christ. For in Him dwells all the fullness of the Godhead bodily; and you are complete in Him, who is the head of all principality and power.

James 1: 16 – 17 Do not be deceived, my beloved brethren. Every good gift and every perfect gift is from above, and comes down from the Father of lights, with whom there is no variation or shadow of turning.

Your take:


165. Buy low and sell high to have a greater gain.

Isaiah 33: 15 – 16 He who walks righteously and speaks uprightly, he who despises the gain of oppressions, who gestures with his hands, refusing bribes, who stops his ears from hearing of bloodshed, and shuts his eyes from seeing evil; he will dwell on high; his place of defense will be the fortress of rocks; bread will be given him, his water will be sure.

Luke 16: 9 – 10 And I say to you, 'make friends for yourselves by unrighteous mammon, that when you fail, they may receive you into an everlasting home. He who is faithful in what is least is faithful also in much; and he who is unjust in what is least is unjust also in much.'

Your take:


166. There is a life changing difference beyond life for those with hope, than for those who are without hope.

Isaiah 57: 19 – 21 "I create the fruit of the lips: Peace, peace to him who is far off and to him who is near," says the Lord, "And I will heal him." But the wicked are like the troubled sea, when it cannot rest, whose waters cast up mire and dirt. "There is no peace," says my God, "For the wicked."

1 Corinthians 9: 9 – 12 For it is written in the law of Moses, "You shall not muzzle an ox while it treads out the grain." Is it oxen God is concerned about? Or does He say it altogether for our sake? For our sakes, no doubt, this is written, that he who plows should plow in hope, and he who threshes in hope should be partaker of his hope. If we have sown spiritual things for you, is it a great thing if we reap your material things? If others are partakers of this right over you, are we not even more?

Your take:


167. Your words are capable of making a friend, or making a foe.

Psalm 41: 9 – 11 Even my own familiar friend in whom I trusted, who ate my bread, has lifted up his heel against me. But You, O Lord, be merciful to me, and raise me up, that I may repay them. By this I know that You are well pleased with me, because my enemy does not triumph over me.

Matthew 26: 48 – 50 Now His betrayer had given them a sign, saying, "Whomever I kiss, He is the One; seize Him." Immediately he went up to Jesus and said, "Greeting, Rabbi!" and kissed Him. But Jesus said to him, "Friend, why have you come?"

Your take:


168. The company you keep can influence how you choose to live and what you do.

Proverbs 13: 20 - 21 He who walks with wise men will be wise, but the companion of fools will be destroyed. Evil pursues sinners, but to the righteous, good shall be repaid.

1 Corinthians 15: 33 – 34 Do not be deceived; "Evil company corrupts good habits." Awake to righteousness, and do not sin; for some do not have the knowledge of God. I speak this to your shame.

Your take:




169. Words given with wisdom and understanding are like a treasured gift.

Psalm 119:27 Make me understand the way of Your precepts; so I shall meditate on Your wonderful works.

Proverbs 25: 11 – 12 A word fitly spoken is like apples of gold in settings of silver. Like an earring of gold and an ornament of fine gold is a wise rebuke to an obedient ear.

Your take:




170. True justice releases the innocent and confines the guilty.

Genesis 18: 17 – 19 And the Lord said, "Shall I hide from Abraham what I am doing, since Abraham shall surely become a great and mighty nation, and all the nations of the earth shall be blessed in him? For I have known him, in order that he may command his children and his household after him, that they keep the way of the Lord, to do righteousness and justice, that the Lord may bring to Abraham what He has spoken to him."

Psalm 9: 8 - 9 He shall judge the world in righteousness, and He shall administer judgement for the peoples in uprightness. The Lord also will be a refuge for the oppressed, a refuge in times of trouble.

Your take:




171. A sunrise is a beginning while a sunset is the end of visible daylight.

Joshua 10: 12 – 13 Then Joshua spoke to the Lord in the day when the Lord delivered up the Amorites before the children of Israel, and he said in the sight of all Israel: "Sun, stand still over Gibeon; and Moon, in the Valley of Aijalon." So the sun stood still, and the moon stopped, till the people had revenge upon their enemies. Is this not written in the Book of Jasher? So the sun stood still in the midst of heaven, and did not hasten to go down for about a whole day.

Acts 2: 20 – 21 The sun shall be turned into darkness, and the moon into blood, before the coming of the great and awesome day of the Lord. And it shall come to pass that whoever calls on the name of the Lord shall be saved.

Your take:


172. The fear of the Lord is the beginning of wisdom.

Genesis 22:12 And He said, "Do not lay your hand on the lad, or do anything to him; for now I know that you fear God, since you have not withheld your son, your only son, from Me."

Psalm 33: 8 – 9 Let all the earth fear the Lord; let all the inhabitants of the world stand in awe of Him. For He spoke, and it was done; He commanded, and it stood fast.

Your take:


173. Hard work enables those to prosper, while laziness leads others to failure.

Proverbs 10: 4 – 5 He who has a slack hand becomes poor, but the hand of the diligent makes rich. He who gathers in summer is a wise son; he who sleeps in harvest is a son who causes shame.

Matthew 25: 26 – 27 But his lord answered and said to him, 'You wicked and lazy servant, you knew that I reap where I have not sown, and gather where I have not scattered seed. So you ought to have deposited my money with the bankers, and at my coming I would have received back my own with interest.'

Your take:


174. Drink water from a clean glass or cup.

Genesis 24: 18 – 19 So she said, "Drink, my lord." Then she quickly let her pitcher down to her hand, and gave him a drink. And when she had finished giving him a drink, she said, "I will draw water for your camels also, until they have finished drinking."

Ruth 2:8 Then Boaz said to Ruth, "You will listen, my daughter, will you not? Do not glean in another field, nor go from here, but stay close by my young women. Let your eyes be on the field which they reap, and go after them. Have I not commanded the young men not to touch you? And when you are thirsty, go to the vessels and drink from what the young men have drawn."

Your take:


175. To prosper from understanding takes action from you.

Proverbs 28:27 He who gives to the poor will not lack, but he who hides his eyes will have many curses.

Acts 13:22 And when He had removed him, He raised up for them David as king, to whom also He gave testimony and said, 'I have found David the son of Jesse, a man after My own heart, who will do all My will.' From this man's seed, according to the promise, God raised up for Israel a Savior – Jesus – after John had first preached, before His coming, the baptism of repentance to all the people of Israel.

Your take:


176. Words from others can either build you up or tear you down.

Psalm 52: 1 – 4 Why do you boast in evil, O mighty man? The goodness of God endures continually. Your tongue devises destruction, like a sharp razor, working deceitfully. You love evil more than good, lying rather than speaking righteousness. You love all devouring words, you deceitful tongue.

Proverbs 15:23 A man has joy by the answer of his mouth, and a word spoken in due season, how good is it!

Your take:


177. Can one walk on hot coals and not be burned?

Proverbs 6: 27 – 29 Can a man take fire to his bosom, and his clothes not be burned? Can one walk on hot coals, and his feet not be seared? So is he who goes in to his neighbor's wife; whoever touches her shall not be innocent.

Romans 12:20 "If your enemy is hungry, feed him; if he is thirsty, give him a drink; for in so doing you will heap coals of fire on his head."

Your take:


178. God told us to build our house, much like our life, on solid ground.

Luke 6:48 He is like a man building a house, who dug deep and laid the foundation on a rock. And when the flood arose, the stream beat vehemently against that house, and could not shake it. For it was founded on the rock.

2 Timothy 2: 20 – 21 But in a great house there are not only vessels of gold and silver, but also of wood and clay, some for honor and some for dishonor. Therefore if anyone cleanses himself from the latter, he will be a vessel for honor, sanctified and useful for the Master, prepared for every good work.

Your take:

179. Forsake foolishness and live the way of understanding.

Luke 11:40 Foolish ones! Did not He who made the outside make the inside also? But rather give alms of such things as you have; then indeed all things are clean to you.

2 Timothy 2: 22 – 23 Flee also youthful lusts; but pursue righteousness, faith, love, peace with those who call on the Lord out of a pure heart. But avoid foolish and ignorant disputes, knowing that they generate strife.

Your take:


180. Sons or daughters who make wise decisions are a tribute to their parents.

Proverbs 10:1 The proverbs of Solomon: a wise son makes a glad father, but a foolish son is the grief of his mother.

Proverbs 23: 24 – 25 The father of the righteous will greatly rejoice, and he who begets a wise child will delight in him. Let your father and your mother be glad, and let her who bore you rejoice.

Your take:


181. Creating dependency and teaching independence are two totally different philosophies.

Acts 17: 22 -25 Then Paul stood in the midst of the Areopagus and said, "Men of Athens, I perceive that in all things you are very religious; for as I was passing through and considering the object of your worship, I found an altar with this inscription: TO THE UNKNOWN GOD. Therefore, the One whom you worship without knowing, Him I proclaim to you: God, who made the world and everything in it, since He is Lord of heaven and earth, does not dwell in temples made with

hands. Nor is He worshiped with men's hands, as though He needed anything, since He gives to all life, breath, and all things."
Your take:

182. God said speak the truth, but do it with love.

Psalm 15: 2 – 5 He who walks uprightly, and works righteousness, and speaks the truth in his heart; he who does not backbite with his tongue, nor does evil to his neighbor, nor does he take up a reproach against his friend; in whose eyes a vile person is despised, but he honors those who fear the Lord; he who swears to his own hurt and does not change; he who does not put out his money at usury, nor does he take a bribe against the innocent. He who does these things shall never be moved.

Your take:

183. A good name chosen is better than choosing riches.

1 Samuel 18:30 Then the princes of the Philistines went out to war. And so it was, whenever they went out, that David behaved more wisely than all the servants of Saul, so that his name became highly esteemed.

2 Samuel 12: 24 – 25 Then David comforted Bathsheba his wife, and went in to her and lay with her. So she bore a son, and he called his name Solomon. Now the Lord loved him, and He sent word by the hand of Nathan the prophet; so he called his name Jedidiah, because of the Lord.

Your take:

184. A wise person who receives knowledge gains more wisdom.

Psalm 90: 12 - 14 So teach us to number our days, that we may gain a heart of wisdom. Return O Lord! How long? And have compassion on Your servants. Oh, satisfy us early with Your mercy, that we may rejoice and be glad all our days!

2 Chronicles 1: 11 – 12 Then God said to Solomon: "Because this was in your heart, and you have not asked riches or wealth or honor or the life of your enemies, nor have you asked for long life – but have asked wisdom and knowledge for yourself, that you may judge My people over whom I have made you king – wisdom and knowledge are granted to you; and I will give you riches and wealth and honor, such as none of the kings have had who were before you, nor shall any after you have the like"

Your take:


185. Gaining wealth through deceit is a short reward.

Proverbs 6: 12 – 15 A worthless person, a wicked man, walks with a perverse mouth; he winks with his eyes, he shuffles his feet, he points with his fingers; perversity is in his heart, he devises evil continually, he sows discord. Therefore his calamity shall come suddenly; suddenly he shall be broken without remedy.

Proverbs 6: 16 – 19 These six things the Lord hates, yes, seven are an abomination to Him; A proud look, a lying tongue, hands that shed blood, a heart that devises wicked plans, feet that are swift in running to evil, a false witness who speaks lies, and one who sows discord among brethren.

Your take:


186. A man who has concern for his neighbors will one day be recognized.

1 Samuel 24: 18 – 19 And you have shown this day how you have dealt well with me; for when the Lord delivered me into your hand, you did not kill me. For if a man finds his enemy, will he let him get

away safely? Therefore may the Lord reward you with good for what you have done to me this day.

Proverbs 11:18 The wicked man does deceptive work, but he who sows righteousness will have a sure reward.

Your take:


187. A borrower is a servant to his lender.

Proverbs 22:7 The rich rules over the poor, and the borrower is servant to the lender.

Nehemiah 5: 9 – 10 Then I said, "What you are doing is not good. Should you not walk in the fear of our God because of the reproach of the nations, our enemies? I also, with my brethren and my servants, am lending them money and grain. Please let us stop this usury!

Your take:


188. Seek the permanent rather than the temporary.

2 Corinthians 4: 17 – 18 For our light affliction, which is but for a moment, is working for us a far more exceeding and eternal weight of glory, while we do not look at the things which are seen, but at the things which are not seen. For the things which are seen are temporary, but the things which are not seen are eternal.

Your take:


189. Do not move permanent survey markers.

Joshua 18:20 The Jordon was its border on the east side. This was the inheritance of the children of Benjamin, according to its boundaries all around, according to their families.

Ezekiel 47:13 Thus says the Lord God, "These are the borders by which you shall divide the land as an inheritance among the twelve tribes of Israel."

Your take:


190. Your words should speak only right things.

1 Samuel 2:3 Talk no more so very proudly; let no arrogance come from your mouth, for the Lord is the God of knowledge; and by Him actions are weighed.

Psalm 17: 4 – 5 Concerning the works of men, by the word of Your lips, I have kept away from the paths of the destroyer. Uphold my steps in Your path, that my footsteps may not slip.

Your take:


191. Be zealous for all that is good.

Numbers 25: 12 – 13 "Therefore say, 'Behold, I give to him My covenant of peace; and it shall be to him and his descendants after him a covenant of an everlasting priesthood, because he was zealous for his God, and made atonement for the children of Israel.' "

Acts 22:3 Then he said: "I am indeed a Jew, born in Tarsus of Cilicia, but brought up in this city at the feet of Gamaliel, taught according to the strictness of our father's law, and was zealous toward God as you are today."

Your take:


192. Diligently receive wisdom, instruction and understanding.

Daniel 9: 22 - 24 And he informed me, and talked with me, and said, "O Daniel, I have now come forth to give you skill to understand. At the beginning of your supplications the command went out, and I have come to tell you, for you are greatly beloved; therefore consider the matter, and understand the vision: Seventy weeks are determined for your people and for your holy city, to finish the transgression, to make an end of sin, to make reconciliation for iniquity, to bring in everlasting righteousness, to seal up vision and prophecy, and to anoint the Most Holy."

Your take:

193. It is good to make your parents proud with your good deeds.

Proverbs 17:6 Children's children are the crown of old men, and the glory of children is their father.

Ephesian 6: 1 – 3 Children, obey your parent in the Lord, for this is right. Honor your father and mother, which is the first commandment with promise; "That it may be well with you and you may live long on the earth."

Your take:

194. Be careful of any politician who offers to buy your vote, but is spending your tax dollars to do it.

Luke 18: 10 – 14 "Two men went up to the temple to pray, one a Pharisee and the other a tax collector. The Pharisee stood and prayed thus with himself, 'God, I thank You that I am not like other men – extortioners, unjust adulterers, or even as this tax collector. I fast twice a week; I give tithes of all that I possess.' And the tax collector, standing afar off, would not so much as raise his eyes to heaven, but beat his breast, saying, 'God, be merciful to me a sinner!' I tell you, this man went down to his house justified rather than the other; for everyone who exalts himself will be humbled, and he who humbles himself will be exalted."

Your take:

195. A wise builder first lays a sound foundation.

Isaiah 58: 11 – 12 The Lord will guide you continually, and satisfy your soul in drought, and strengthen your bones; you shall be like a watered garden, and like a spring of water, whose waters do not fail. Those from among you shall build the old waste places; you shall raise up the foundations of many generations; and you shall be called the repairer of the breach, the restorer of streets to dwell in.

1 Corinthians 3: 10 – 11 According to the grace of God which was given to me, as a wise master builder I have laid the foundation, and another builds on it. But let each one take heed how he builds on it. For no other foundation can anyone lay than that which is laid, which is Jesus Christ.

Your take:


196. Realize that God knows even the count of the hairs on your head.

Genesis 15:5 Then He brought him outside and said, "Look now toward heaven, and count the stars if you are able to number them" And He said to him, "So shall your descendants be."

Psalm 69:4 Those who hate me without a cause are more than the hairs of my head; they are mighty who would destroy me, being my enemies wrongfully; though I have stolen nothing, I still must restore it.

Luke 12: 6 – 7 Are not five sparrows sold for two copper coins? And not one of them is forgotten before God. But the very hairs of your head are all numbered. Do not fear therefore; you are of more value than many sparrows.

Your take:

197. He who plots to do evil is called a schemer.

Proverbs 21:12 The righteous God wisely considers the house of the wicked, overthrowing the wicked for their wickedness.

Ecclesiastes 8: 11 - 13 Because the sentence against an evil work is not executed speedily, therefore the heart of the sons of men is fully set in them to do evil. Though a sinner does evil a hundred times, and his days are prolonged, yet I surely know that it will be well with those who fear God, who fear before Him.

Your take:


198. Always desire to please your Maker.

Psalm 41: 11 – 12 By this I know that You are well pleased with me, because my enemy does not triumph over me. As for me, You uphold me in my integrity, and set me before Your face forever.

Micah 6:8 He has shown you, O man, what is good; and what does the Lord require of you but to do justly, to love mercy, and to walk humbly with your God?

Your take:


199. The fear of the Lord is the beginning of wisdom.

Deuteronomy 10: 20 – 21 You shall fear the Lord your God; you shall serve Him, and to Him you shall hold fast, and take oaths in His name. He is your praise, and He is your God, who has done for you these great and awesome things which your eyes have seen.

Your take:


200. Eating more than you should may make you sick.

Proverbs 23:21 For the drunkard and the glutton will come to poverty, and drowsiness will clothe a man with rags.

Luke 7:34 - 35 The Son of Man has come eating and drinking, and you say, 'Look, a glutton and a winebibber, a friend of tax collectors and sinners!' But wisdom is justified by all her children.

Proverbs 28:7 Whoever keeps the law is a discerning son, but a companion of gluttons shames his father.

Your take:


201. God said love your enemy, feed him and give him drink. Your rewards come later.

Proverbs 16:7 When a man's ways please the Lord, He makes even his enemies to be at peace with him.

Matthew 5: 43 – 45 You have heard that it was said, 'You shall love your neighbor and hate your enemy, but I say to you, love your enemies, bless those who curse you, do good to those who hate you, and pray for those who spitefully use you and persecute you, that you may be sons of your Father in heaven; for He makes His sun rise on the evil, and on the good, and sends rain on the just and on the unjust.

Your take:


202. Your life may have all of these at various times, love, laughter, and peace, as well as, loneliness, sorrow, and turmoil.

Proverbs 14:13 Even in laughter the heart may sorrow, and the end of mirth may be grief.

James 4: 8 – 9 Draw near to God and He will draw near to you. Cleanse your hands, you sinners; and purify your hearts, you double-minded. Lament and mourn and weep! Let your laughter be turned to mourning and your joy to gloom. Humble yourselves in the sight of the Lord, and He will lift you up.

Your take:

203. It is better to mind your own business, and not that of others.

Ecclesiastes 4:8 There is one alone, without companion: He has neither son nor brother. Yet there is no end to all his labors, nor is his eye satisfied with riches. But he never asks, "For whom do I toil and deprive myself of good?" This also is vanity and a grave misfortune.

1 Corinthians 5: 12 – 13 For what have I to do with judging those also who are outside? Do you not judge those who are inside? But those who are outside God judges. Therefore "put away from yourselves the evil person."

Your take:


204. It is better to have a good neighbor close by than a brother far away.

Proverbs 3: 28 – 30 Do not say to your neighbor, "Go, and come back, and tomorrow I will give it." When you have it with you. Do not devise evil against your neighbor, for he dwells by you for safety's sake. Do not strive with a man without cause, if he has done you no harm.

Romans 13:10 Love does no harm to a neighbor; therefore love is the fulfillment of the law.

Your take:


205. You can't take your things with you when your life ends.

Job 20:28 – 29 The increase of his house will depart, and his goods will flow away in the day of His wrath. This is the portion from God for a wicked man, the heritage appointed to him by God.

Luke 12: 33 – 34 Sell what you have and give alms; provide yourselves money bags which do not grow old, a treasure in the heavens that does not fail, where no thief approaches nor moth destroys. For where your treasure is, there your heart will be also.

Your take:

206. If you're willing to work you should never go hungry.

Proverbs 19: 15 Laziness cast one into a deep sleep, and an idle person will suffer hunger.

Philippians 4: 12 – 13 I know how to be abased, and I know how to abound. Everywhere and in all things I have learned both to be full and to be hungry, both to abound and to suffer need. I can do all things through Christ who strengthens me.

Your take:

207. God said to be swift to hear, slow to speak and slow to wrath.

Proverbs 15: 1 – 2 A soft answer turns away wrath, but a harsh word stirs up anger. The tongue of the wise uses knowledge rightly, but the mouth of fools pours forth foolishness.

James 1: 19 - 20 So then, my beloved brethren, let every man be swift to hear, slow to speak, slow to wrath; for the wrath of man does not produce the righteousness of God.

Your take:

208. Land without rain yields little gain, much like words without truth.

Exodus 18: 24 – 25 So Moses heeded the voice of his father-in-law and did all that he had said. And Moses chose able men out of all Israel, and made them heads over the people: rulers of thousands, rulers of hundreds, rulers of fifties, and rulers of tens.

Proverbs 16:8 Better is a little with righteousness, than vast revenues without justice.

Isaiah 5:6 "I will lay it waste; it shall not be pruned or dug, but there shall come up briers and thorns. I will also command the clouds that they rain no rain on it."

Your take:

209. Whenever possible live peacefully with all around you.

Romans 12: 18 – 19 If it is possible, as much as depends on you, live peaceable with all men. Beloved, do not avenge yourselves, but rather give place to wrath; for it is written, "Vengeance is Mine, I will repay," says the Lord.

Your take:

210. When all of your tomorrows are secure, peace and joy rein in all your todays.

Psalm 4:8 I will both lie down in peace, and sleep; for You alone, O Lord, make me dwell in safety.

Proverbs 3: 13 – 15 Happy is the man who finds wisdom, and the man who gains understanding; for her proceeds are better than the profits of silver, and her gain than fine gold. She is more precious than rubies, and all the things you may desire cannot compare with her.

Your take:

211. Why do we reward those who fail to try, but punish those who work hard to succeed?

Luke 16: 25 – 26 But Abraham said, 'Son, remember that in your lifetime you received your good things, and likewise Lazarus evil things; but now he is comforted and you are tormented. And besides all this, between us and you there is a great gulf fixed, so that those who want to pass from here to you cannot, nor can those from there pass to us.'

Your take:


212. Tomorrow is an unknown because we haven't arrived there yet.

Joshua 3: 5 – 6 And Joshua said to the people, "Sanctify yourselves, for tomorrow the Lord will do wonders among you." Then Joshua spoke to the priests, saying, "Take up the Ark of the Covenant and cross over before the people."

2 Chronicles 20:17 'You will not need to fight in this battle. Position yourselves, stand still and see the salvation of the Lord, who is with you, O Judah and Jerusalem!'

Mathew 6:34 Therefore do not worry about tomorrow, for tomorrow will worry about its own things. Sufficient for the day is its own trouble.

Your take:


213. Tell them who spend your tax dollars that lower taxes leaves us with more spendable money, which leads to more commerce.

Luke 23: 2 – 4 And they began to accuse Him, saying, "We found this fellow perverting the nation, and forbidding to pay taxes to Caesar, saying that He Himself is Christ, a King." Then Pilate asked Him, saying, "Are You the King of the Jews?" He answered him and said, "It is as you say." So Pilate said to the chief priests and the crowd, "I find no fault in this Man."

Romans 13: 7 – 8 Render therefore to all their due; taxes to whom taxes are due, customs to whom customs, fear to whom fear, honor to whom honor.

Your take:

214. Seek God daily, not just when trouble finds you.

2 Chronicles 7: 14 – 15 If My people who are called by My name will humble themselves, and pray and seek My face, and turn from their wicked ways, then I will hear from heaven, and will forgive their sin and heal their land. Now My eyes will be open and My ears attentive to prayer made in this place.

Hebrews 11:6 But without faith it is impossible to please Him, for he who comes to God must believe that He is, and that He is a rewarder of those who diligently seek Him.

Your take:


215. Always speak the truth to avoid causing destruction of the innocent.

Exodus 23: 6 – 7 "You shall not pervert the judgement of your poor in his dispute. Keep yourself far from a false matter; do not kill the innocent and righteous. For I will not justify the wicked."

Isaiah 5:23 Who justify the wicked for a bribe, and take away justice from the righteous man!

James 5: 5 – 6 You have lived on the earth in pleasure and luxury; you have fattened your hearts as in a day of slaughter. You have condemned, you have murdered the just; he does not resist you.

Your take:


216. Marriage is God's first institution and His plan for creating families.

Genesis 2: 20 – 24 So Adam gave names to all cattle, to the birds of the air, and to every beast of the field. But for Adam there was not found a helper comparable to him. And the Lord God caused a deep sleep to fall on Adam, and he slept; and He took one of his ribs, and closed up the flesh in its place. Then the rib which the Lord God had taken from man He made into a woman, and He brought her to the man. And Adam said: "This is now bone of my bones and flesh of my flesh; she shall be called woman, because she was taken out of man." Therefore a man shall leave his father and mother and be joined to his wife, and they shall become one flesh.

Your take:


217. Driving recklessly and walking on thin ice have much in common.

Isaiah 59:10 We grope for the wall like the blind, and we grope as if we had no eyes; we stumble at noonday as at twilight; we are as dead men in desolate places.

John 12: 35 – 36 Then Jesus said to them, "A little while longer the light is with you. Walk while you have the light, lest darkness overtake you; he who walks in darkness does not know where he is going. While you have the light, believe in the light, that you may become sons of light." These things Jesus spoke, and departed, and was hidden from them.

Your take:


218. Most rainbows appear after a daytime rain shower.

Genesis 9: 16 – 17 "The rainbow shall be in the cloud, and I will look on it to remember the everlasting covenant between God and every living creature of all flesh that is on the earth." And God said to Noah, "This is the sign of the covenant which I have established between Me and all flesh that is on the earth."

Your take:

219. Peace and strife can be found in the house of both the rich and of the poor.

Psalm 120: 6 – 7 My soul has dwelt too long with one who hates peace. I am for peace; but when I speak, they are for war.

Proverbs 17:1 Better is a dry morsel with quietness, than a house full of feasting with strife.

Your take:


220. Everyone has their place rained on at times.

Psalm 72:6 – 7 He shall come down like rain upon the grass before mowing, like showers that water the earth. In His days the righteous shall flourish, and abundance of peace, until the moon is no more.

Acts 28:2 And the natives showed us unusual kindness; for they kindled a fire and made us all welcome, because of the rain that was falling and because of the cold.

Your take:


221. Always treat your neighbors like you want them to treat you.

Luke 10: 36 – 37 "So which of these three do you think was neighbor to him who fell among the thieves?" And he said, "He who showed mercy on him." Then Jesus said to him, "Go and do likewise."

Romans 13:10 Love does no harm to a neighbor; therefore love is the fulfillment of the law.

Romans 15:2 Let each of us please his neighbor for his good, leading to edification.

Your take:


222. Let's work towards putting UNITED back in the UNITED STATES of AMERICA.

Psalm 133:1 Behold, how good and how pleasant it is for brethren to dwell together in unity!

Colossians 3:17 And whatever you do in word or deed, do all in the name of the Lord Jesus, giving thanks to God the Father through Him.

You take:


223. Fallen leaves should be raked down wind.

2 Chronicles 24:12 The King and Jehoiada gave it to those who did the work of the service of the house of the Lord; and they hired masons and carpenters to repair the house of the Lord, and also those who worked in iron and bronze to restore the house of the Lord.

Proverbs 22:29 Do you see a man who excels in his work? He will stand before kings; he will not stand before unknown men.

Your take:


224. We are not a machine, we have emotion, and greater than that, we have compassion, and we have a soul.

Joshua 22: 5 -6 "But take careful heed to do the commandment and the law which Moses the servant of the Lord commanded you, to love the Lord your God, to walk in all his ways, to keep His commandments, to hold fast to Him, and to serve Him with all your heart and with all your soul." So Joshua blessed them and sent them away, and they went to their tents.

Matthew 22: 37 – 39 Jesus said to him, "'You shall love the Lord your God with all your heart, with all your soul, and with all your mind.' This is the first and great commandment. And the second is like it: You shall love your neighbor as yourself.' On these two commandments hang all the Law and the Prophets."

Your take:

225. A reminder, what you share in confidence can be spread around without your permission.

Proverbs 11:13 A talebearer reveals secrets, but he who is of a faithful spirit conceals a matter.

1 Timothy 5:13 And besides they learn to be idle, wandering about from house to house, and not only idle but also gossips and busybodies, saying things which they ought not.

Your take:


226. Life is too short to worry about the unimportant things.

Mark 4: 18 – 19 Now these are the ones sown among thorns; they are the ones who hear the word, and the cares of this world, the deceitfulness of riches, and the desires for other things entering in choke the word, and it becomes unfruitful.

Luke 10: 41 – 42 And Jesus answered and said to her, "Martha, Martha, you are worried and troubled about many things. But one thing is needed, and Mary has chosen that good part, which will not be taken away from her."

Your take:


227. God told us that to worry is a sin.

Psalm 32:4 – 5 For day and night Your hand was heavy upon me; my vitality was turned into the drought of summer. I acknowledge my sin to You. And my iniquity I have not hidden. I said, "I will confess my transgressions to the Lord," and You forgave the iniquity of my sin.

Matthew 6: 27 - 28 Which of you by worrying can add one cubit to his stature? So why do you worry about clothing? Consider the lilies of the field, how they grow: they neither toil nor spin; and yet I say to you that even Solomon in all his glory was not arrayed like one of these.

Your take:

228. While we live, the rest of our story has not been told yet.

Joshua 21:2 And they spoke to them at Shiloh in the land of Canaan, saying, "The Lord commanded through Moses to give us cities to dwell in, with their common-lands for our livestock."

Ecclesiastes 3: 12 – 13 I know that nothing is better for them than to rejoice, and to do good in their lives and also that every man should eat and drink and enjoy the good of all his labor – it is the gift of God.

Your take:

229. Some plow, some sow and some water, but God makes it all grow.

1 Corinthians 3:7 - 9 So then neither he who plants is anything, nor he who waters, but God who gives the increase. Now he who plants and he who waters are one, and each one will receive his own reward according to his own labor. For we are God's fellow workers; you are God's field, you are God's building.

Your take:

230. In some geographic areas swimming and ice skating can be done in the same place depending on the season.

Ecclesiastes 3: 1 – 8 To everything there is a season, a time for every purpose under heaven; a time to be born, and a time to die; a time to plant, and a time to pluck what is planted; a time to kill, and a time to heal; a time to break down, and a time to build up; a time to weep, and a time to laugh; a time to mourn, and a time to dance; a time to cast away stones, and a time to gather stones; a time to embrace, and a time to refrain from embracing; a time to gain, and a time to lose; a time to keep, and a time to throw away; a time to tear; and a time to sew; a time to keep silence, and a time to speak; a time to love, and a time to hate; a time to war, and a time of peace.

Your take:

231. Things done in secret often get brought out in the open.

Psalm 90:8 You have set our iniquities before You, our secret sins in light of your countenance.

Ephesians 5: 12 – 14 For it is shameful even to speak of those things which are done by them in secret. But all things that are exposed are made manifest by the light, for whatever makes manifest is light. Therefore He says: "Awake, you who sleep, arise from the dead, and Christ will give you light."

Your take:

232. We may not like to admit it but we are all guilty of something.

1 John 2: 1 – 2 My little children, these things I write to you, so that you may not sin. And if anyone sins, we have an Advocate with the Father, Jesus Christ the righteous. And He Himself is the propitiation for our sins, and not for ours only but also for the whole world.

Your take:

233. Be careful what you speak or write today, they may be questioned one day.

Joshua 23: 6 – 8 Therefore be very courageous to keep and to do all that is written in the Book of the Law of Moses, lest you turn aside from it to the right hand or to the left, and lest you go among these nations, these who remain among you. You shall not make mention of the name of their gods, nor cause anyone to swear by them; you shall not serve them nor bow down to them, but you shall hold fast to the Lord your God, as you have done to this day.

Luke 21:36 "Watch therefore, and pray always that you may be counted worthy to escape all these things that will come to pass, and to stand before the Son of Man."

Your take:

234. Time, like money should be spent wisely.

Isaiah 58:10 If you extend your soul to the hungry and satisfy the afflicted soul, then your light shall dawn in the darkness, and your darkness shall be as the noonday.

Acts 18: 20 – 21 When they asked him to stay a longer time with them, he did not consent, but took leave of them, saying, "I must by all means keep this coming feast in Jerusalem; but I will return again to you, God willing." And he sailed from Ephesus.

Your take:

235. When everything you tried failed, why didn't you seek God's wisdom first?

Leviticus 19: 30 – 31 'You shall keep My Sabbaths and reverence My sanctuary: I am the Lord. Give no regard to mediums and familiar spirits; do not seek after them, to be defiled by them: I am the Lord your God.

2 Chronicles 14: 2 – 4 Asa did what was good and right in the eyes of the Lord his God, for he removed the altars of the foreign gods and the high places, and broke down the sacred pillars and cut down the wooden images. He commanded Judah to seek the Lord God of their fathers, and to observe the law and the commandment.

Your take:

236. Correct numbers are needed to balance any project.

Jeremiah 11: 6 - 7 Then the Lord said to me, "Proclaim all these words in the cities of Judah and in the streets of Jerusalem, saying, 'Hear the words of this covenant and do them. For I earnestly exhorted your fathers in the day I brought them up out of the land of Egypt, until this day, rising up early and exhorting, saying: "Obey My voice."

2 Timothy 4: 2 – 4 Preach the word! Be ready in season and out of season. Convince, rebuke, exhort, with all longsuffering and teaching. For the time will come when they will not endure sound doctrine, but according to their own desires, because they have itching ears, they will heap up for themselves teachers; and they will turn their ears away from the truth, and be turned aside to fables.

Your take:


237. Farming is like chess, get the most gain from the least number of wise moves.

Ecclesiastes 7: 11 – 13 Wisdom is good with an inheritance, and profitable to those who see the sun. For wisdom is a defense as money is a defense, but the excellence of knowledge is that wisdom gives life to those who have it. Consider the work of God; for who can make straight what He has made crooked?

Jeremiah 31:5 You shall yet plant vines on the mountains of Samaria; the planters shall plant and eat them as ordinary food.

Your take:


238. Clean water is the best drink of choice.

1 Kings 13: 16 – 17 And he said, "I cannot return with you nor go in with you; neither can I eat bread nor drink water with you in this

place. For I have been told by the word of the Lord, 'You shall not eat bread nor drink water there, nor return by going the way you came.'"

John 4: 9 – 10 Then the woman of Samaria said to Him, "How is it that You, being a Jew, ask a drink from me, a Samaritan woman?" For Jews have no dealings with Samaritans. Jesus answered and said to her, "If you knew the gift of God, and who it is who says to you, 'Give me a drink,' you would have asked Him, and He would have given you living water."

Your take:

239. Be aware, your children often mimic your actions.

Hebrews 6: 11 – 12 And we desire that each one of you show the same diligence to the full assurance of hope until the end, that you do not become sluggish, but imitate those who through faith and patience inherit the promises.

3 John 1:11 Beloved, do not imitate what is evil, but what is good. He who does good is of God, but he who does evil has not seen God.

Your take:

240. Future glory is waiting for you, look before you leap.

Psalm 28:7 The Lord is my strength and my shield; my heart trusted in Him, and I am helped; therefore my heart greatly rejoices, and with my song I will praise Him.

Isaiah 35: 9 – 10 No lion shall be there, nor shall any ravenous beast go up on it; it shall not be found there. But the redeemed shall walk there, and the ransomed of the Lord shall return, and come to Zion with singing, with everlasting joy on their heads. They shall obtain joy and gladness, and sorrow and sighing shall flee away.

Your take:

241. A few hours of research can save you untold amounts of wasted actions.

Ecclesiastes 1: 13 – 15 And I set my heart to seek and search out by wisdom concerning all that is done under heaven; this burdensome task God has given to the sons of man, by which they may be exercised. I have seen all the works that are done under the sun; and indeed, all is vanity and grasping for the wind. What is crooked cannot be made straight, and what is lacking cannot be numbered.

John 7: 15 – 16 And the Jews marveled, saying, "How does this Man know letters, having never studied?" Jesus answered them and said. "My doctrine is not Mine, but His who sent Me. If anyone wills to do His will, he shall know concerning the doctrine, whether it is from God or whether I speak on My own authority."

Your take:


242. Work is like chess, correctly spend the least energy to get the most accomplished.

2 Chronicles 15: 8 – 9 And when Asa heard these words and the prophecy of Oded the prophet, he took courage, and removed the abominable idols from all the land of Judah and Benjamin and from the cities which he had taken in the mountains of Ephraim; and he restored the altar of the Lord that was before the vestibule of the Lord. Then he gathered all Judah and Benjamin, and those who dwelt with them from Ephraim, Manasseh, and Simeon, for they came over to him in great numbers from Israel when they saw that the Lord his God was with him.

Ecclesiastes 3:17 I said in my heart, "God shall judge the righteous and the wicked, for there is a time there for every purpose and for every work."

Your take:

243. One person's junk may be great treasure to an artist.Isaiah 44: 9 - 10 Those who make an image, all of them are useless. And their precious things shall not profit; they are their own witnesses; they neither see nor know, that they may be ashamed. Who would form a god or mold an image that profits him nothing?

Your take:


244. A little thought, a little planning, along with a little effort from a great number of people can complete a huge project.

Ecclesiastes 2:21 + 24 For there is a man whose labor is with wisdom, knowledge, and skill; yet he must leave his heritage to a man who has not labored for it. This also is vanity and a great evil. (Plus) Nothing is better for a man than that he should eat and drink, and that his soul should enjoy good in his labor. This also, I saw, was from the hand of God.

Your take:


245. God gave His people the land flowing with milk and honey, and He gave to us our GREAT USA, OUR COUNTRY.

Exodus 13:5 And it shall be when the Lord brings you into the land of the Canaanites and the Hittites and the Amorites and the Hivites and the Jebusites, which He swore to your fathers to give you, a land flowing with milk and honey, that you shall keep this service in this month.

Your take:

246. Your words of instruction spoken may get little results, but show and tell can have greater benefit.

Matthew 13: 33 Another parable He spoke to them: "The kingdom of heaven is like leaven, which a woman took and hid in three measures of meal till it was all leavened."

Luke 5:36 Then He spoke a parable to them: "No one puts a piece from a new garment on an old one; otherwise the new makes a tear, and also the piece that was taken out of the new does not match the old."

Your take:


247. The Gospel means Good News, read it and find out how true it really is.

Isaiah 61: 1 – 3 "The Spirit of the Lord God is upon Me, because the Lord has anointed Me to preach good tidings to the poor; He has sent Me to heal the brokenhearted, to proclaim liberty to the captives, and the opening of the prison to those who are bound; to proclaim the acceptable year of the Lord, and the day of vengeance of our God; to comfort all who mourn, to console those who mourn in Zion, to give them beauty for ashes, the oil of joy for mourning, the garment of praise for the spirit of heaviness, the planting of the Lord, that He may be glorified."

Your take:


248. Wise investment of your money and time normally brings huge dividends.

Genesis 41:48 So he gathered up all the food of the seven years which were in the land of Egypt, and laid up the food in the cities; he laid up in every city the food of the fields which surrounded them. Joseph gathered very much grain, as the sand of the sea, until he stopped counting, for it was immeasurable.

Your take:

249. Interest paid is funds spent, interest earned is funds gained.

Deuteronomy 23: 19 - 20 "You shall not charge interest to your brother- interest on money for food or anything that is lent out at interest. To the foreigner you may charge interest, that the Lord your God may bless you in all to which you set your hand in the land which you are entering to possess."

Matthew 25: 27 - 28 "So you ought to have deposited my money with the bankers, and at my coming I would have received back my own with interest. So take the talent from him, and give it to him who has ten talents."

Your take:


250. There is a place to cast all your cares on.

Psalm 55:22 Cast your burden on the Lord, and He shall sustain you; He shall never permit the righteous to be moved.

1 Peter 5: 6 – 7 Therefore humble yourselves under the mighty hand of God, that He may exalt you in due time, casting all your care upon Him, for He cares for you.

Your take:


251. God said to love your neighbor, even if it may be hard to do.

Romans 13:9 - 10 For the commandments, "You shall not commit adultery," "You shall not murder," "You shall not steal," "You shall not bear false witness," "You shall not covet," and if there is any other commandment, are all summed up in this saying, namely, "You shall love your neighbor as yourself." Love does no harm to a neighbor; therefore love is the fulfillment of the law.

Your take:

252. A word spoken can't be erased.

Deuteronomy 7: 7 – 8 The Lord did not set His love on you nor choose you because you were more in number than any other people, for you were the least of all people; but because the Lord loves you, and because He would keep the oath which He swore to your fathers, the Lord has brought you out with a mighty hand, and redeemed you from the house of bondage, from the hand of Pharaoh king of Egypt.

John 12:26 If anyone serves Me, let him follow Me; and where I am, there My servant will be also. If anyone serves Me, him My Father will honor.

Your take:


253. A picture without a frame is like a book without its cover.

Psalm 139: 15 – 16 My frame was not hidden from You, when I was made in secret, and skillfully wrought in the lowest parts of the earth. Your eyes saw my substance, being yet unformed. And in Your book they all were written, the days fashioned for me, when as yet there were none of them.

Isaiah 58: 13 – 14 "If you turn away your foot from the Sabbath, from doing your pleasure on My holy day, and call the Sabbath a delight, the holy day of the Lord honorable, and shall honor Him, not doing your own ways, nor finding your own pleasure, nor speaking your own words, then you shall delight yourself in the Lord; and I will cause you to ride on the high hills of the earth, and feed you with the heritage of Jacob your father. The mouth of the Lord as spoken."

Your take:


254. Hiding an item in a box, it is out of sight and out of mind.

Ezekiel 39: 23 – 24 "The Gentiles shall know that the house of Israel went into captivity for their iniquity; because they were unfaithful to Me, therefore I hid My face from them. I gave them into the hand of their enemies, and they all fell by the sword. According to their uncleanness and according to their transgressions I have dealt with them, and hidden My face from them."

Matthew 10:27 "Whatever I tell you in the dark, speak in the light; and what you hear in the ear, preach on the housetops. And do not fear those who kill the body but cannot kill the soul. But rather fear Him who is able to destroy both the soul and the body in hell."

Your take:


255. Believe it or not, your phone should be a tool in your hand, not your companion.

Acts 22: 10 - 11 So I said, "What shall I do, Lord?" And the Lord said to me, "Arise and go into Damascus, and there you will be told all things which are appointed for you to do." And since I could not see for the glory of that light, being led by the hand of those who were with me, I came into Damascus.

Hebrews 1:8 – 9 But to the Son He says, "Your throne, O God, is forever and ever; A scepter of righteousness is the scepter of Your kingdom. You have loved righteousness and hated lawlessness; therefore God, Your God, has anointed You with the oil of gladness more than Your companions."

Your take:


256. Why defund? Why completely give up your safety because of a very few bad protectors?

Zephaniah 3: 1 – 3 Woe to her who is rebellious and polluted, to the oppressing city! She has not obeyed His voice, she has not received correction; she has not trusted in the Lord, she has not drawn near to her God. Her princes in her midst are roaring lions; Her judges are evening wolves that leave not a bone till morning.

1 Thessalonian 5: 3 – 6 For when they say, "Peace and safety!" then sudden destruction comes upon them, as labor pains upon a pregnant woman. And they shall not escape. But you, brethren, are not in darkness, so that this Day should overtake you as a thief. You are all sons of light and sons of the day. We are not of the night nor of darkness. Therefore let us not sleep, as others do, but let us watch and be sober.

Your take:


257. To neglect moderation tips the scales of life in the wrong direction.

2 Samuel 22: 26 – 27 With the merciful You show Yourself merciful; with the blameless man You will show Yourself blameless; with the pure You will show Yourself pure; and with the devious You will show Yourself shrewd.

Psalm 18: 27 – 30 For You will save the humble people, but will bring down haughty looks. For You will light my lamp; the Lord my God will enlighten my darkness. For by You I can run against a troop, by my God I can leap over a wall. As for God, His way is perfect; the word of the Lord is proven; He is a shield to all who trust in Him.

Your take:


258. Staying faithful to God is a huge part of staying healthy.

Proverbs 3: 5 – 8 Trust in the Lord with all your heart, and lean not on your own understanding; in all your ways acknowledge Him, and He shall direct your paths. Do not be wise in your own eyes; fear the

Lord and depart from evil. It will be health to your flesh, and strength to your bones.

3 John 1: 2 - 4 Beloved, I pray that you may prosper in all things and be in health, just as your soul prospers. For I rejoiced greatly when brethren came and testified of the truth that is in you, just as you walk in the truth. I have no greater joy than to hear that my children walk in truth.

Your take:


259. Drinking plenty of clean water daily are recommended to help maintain good health.

Genesis 24: 11 – 14 And he made his camels kneel down outside the city by a well of water at evening time, the time when women go out to draw water. The he said, "O Lord God of my master Abraham, please give me success this day, and show kindness to my master Abraham. Behold, here I stand by the well of water, and the daughters of the men of the city are coming out to draw water. Now let it be that the young woman to whom I say, 'Please let down your pitcher that I may drink,' and she says, 'Drink, and I will also give your camels a drink; - let her be the one You have appointed for Your servant Isaac, And by this I will know that You have shown kindness to my master."

Your take:


260. A good balance is key to most everything.

Psalm 62: 11 – 12 God has spoken once, twice I have heard this: That power belongs to God. Also to you, O Lord, belongs mercy, for You render to each one according to his work.

Isaiah 40: 12 – 13 Who has measured the waters in the hollow of His hand, measured heaven with a span and calculated the dust of the earth in a measure? Weighed the mountains in scales and the hills in a balance? Who has directed the Spirit of the Lord, or as His counselor has taught Him?

Your take:


261. God said all things are acceptable in moderation, but I say some things are not practical.

Proverbs 21:3 To do righteousness and justice is more acceptable to the Lord than sacrifice.

2 Corrinthians 8:12 For if there is first a willing mind, it is accepted according to what one has, and not according to what he does not have.

Your take:


262. Ongoing prayer early and at the end of the day brings us closer to our creator, and reminds us Who is really in control.

1 Chronicles 29: 10 – 12 Therefore David blessed the Lord before all the assembly; and David said, "Blessed are You, Lord God of Israel, our Father, forever and ever. Yours, O Lord, is the greatness, the power and the glory, the victory and the majesty; for all that is in heaven and in earth is Yours; Yours is the kingdom, O Lord, and You are exalted as head over all. Both riches and honor come from You, and You reign over all. In your hand is power and might; in Your hand it is to make great and to give strength to all."

Your take:


263. Good health is not only a good physical, but also a good mental and a good spiritual condition.

Psalm 39: 12 – 13 "Hear my prayer, O Lord, and give ear to my cry; do not be silent at my tears; for I am a stranger with You, a sojourner, as all my fathers were. Remove Your gaze from me, that I may regain strength, before I go away and am no more."

Isaiah 38: 15 – 17 "What shall I say? He has both spoken to me, and He Himself has done it. I shall walk carefully all my years in the bitterness of my soul. O Lord, by these things men live; and in all these things is the life of my spirit; so You will restore me and make me live. Indeed it was for my own peace that I had great bitterness; but You have lovingly delivered my soul from the pit of corruption, for You have cast all my sins behind Your back."

Your take:


264. God told us, "Peace I give to you, not as the world gives, I give to you." Seek His peace today.

1 Chronicles 16: 10 – 13 Glory in His holy name; let the hearts of those rejoice who seek the Lord! Seek the Lord and His strength; seek His face evermore! Remember His marvelous works which He has done, His wonders, and the judgment of His mouth, O seed of Israel His servant, you children of Jacob, His chosen ones!

Isaiah 66: 12 – 13 For thus says the Lord, "Behold, I will extend peace to her like a river, and the glory of the Gentiles like a flowing stream. Then you shall feed; on her sides shall you be carried, and be dangled on her knees. As on whom his mother comforts, so I will comfort you; and you shall be comforted in Jerusalem."

Your take:


265. The Lord went about healing the sick, the lame, and the blind, and He also is able to calm the external and internal storms.

Psalm 89: 8 – 9 O Lord God of hosts, Who is mighty like You, O Lord? Your faithfulness also surrounds You. You rule the raging of the sea; when its waves rise, You still them.

Mathew 4: 23 – 24 And Jesus went about all Galilee, teaching in their synagogues, preaching the gospel of the kingdom, and healing all kinds sickness and all kinds of disease among the people. Then His fame went throughout all Syria; and they brought to Him all sick people who were afflicted with various diseases and torments, and those who were demon-possessed, epileptics, and paralytics; and He healed them.

Your take:


266. Make a reasonable plan for tomorrow before you find your pillow tonight, leaving time for all the important things you want to accomplish then.

Joshua 3: 5 – 6 And Joshua said to the people, "Sanctify yourselves, for tomorrow the Lord will do wonders among you." Then Joshua spoke to the priests, saying, "Take up the Ark of the Covenant and cross over before the people."

Joshua 11:23 So Joshua took the whole land, according to all that the Lord had said to Moses; and Joshua gave it as an inheritance to Israel according to their divisions by their tribes. Then the land rested from war.

Your take:


267. To some a cloud is a filter of the bright hot sun, to others it is a miracle bringing moisture, and cooling winds for growth.

Numbers 9: 15 – 16 Now on the day that the tabernacle was raised up, the cloud covered the tabernacle, and the tent of the Testimony; from evening until morning it was above the tabernacle like the appearance of fire. So it was always: the cloud covered it by day, and the appearance of fire by night.

Mathew 17: 5 - 6 While he was still speaking, behold a bright cloud overshadowed them; and suddenly a voice came out of the cloud, saying, "This is My beloved Son, in whom I am will pleased. Hear Him!" And when the disciples heard it, they fell on their faces and were greatly afraid.

Your take:



268. Whatever happens revealing deep emotions reveals one's true heart condition.

Mathew 12: 49 – 50 And He stretched out His hand toward His disciples and said, "Here are My mother and My brothers! For whoever does the will of My father in heaven is My brother and sister and mother."

John 5: 6 – 7 When Jesus saw him lying there, and knew that he already had been in that condition a long time, He said to him, "Do you want to be made well?" The sick man answered Him, "Sir, I have no man to put me into the pool when the water is stirred up; But while I am coming, another steps down before me."

Your take:



269. Toleration, patience, forbearance should NOT be only a one way street, but SHOULD always be two ways.

Psalm 14: 1 – 4 The fool has said in his heart, "There is no God." They are corrupt, they have done abominable works, there is none who does good. The Lord looks down from heaven upon the children of men, to see if there are any who understand, who seek God. They have together become corrupt; there is none who does good, no not one. Have all the workers of iniquity no knowledge, who eat up my people as they eat bread, and do not call on the Lord?

Romans 1: 16 – 17 For I am not ashamed of the gospel of Christ, for it is the power of God to salvation for everyone who believes, for the Jew first and also for the Greek. For in it the righteousness of God is revealed from faith to faith; as it is written, "The just shall live by faith."
Your take:

270. A smile reflects light, while a frown reflects darkness.
2 Samuel 22:29 For You are my lamp, O Lord; the Lord shall enlighten my darkness.
Psalm 107: 14 – 15 He brought them out of darkness and the shadow of death, and broke their chains in pieces. Oh, that men would give thanks to the Lord for His goodness, and for His wonderful works to the children of men!
Your take:

271. An insult from others can be dealt with by building on, or in contrast, being willing to forgive their indiscretion.
Psalm 69: 8 – 9 I have become a stranger to my brothers, and an alien to my mother's children; because zeal for Your house has eaten me up, and the reproaches of those who reproach You have fallen on me.
Luke 6: 22 – 23 Blessed are you when men hate you, and when they exclude you, and revile you, and cast out your name as evil, for the Son of Man's sake. Rejoice in that day and leap for joy! For indeed your reward is great in heaven, for in like manner their fathers did to the prophets.
Your take:

272. Most any good or bad decisions you make today can have lifelong effects.

2 Samuel 15: 3 - 4 Then Absalom would say to him, "Look, your case is good and right; but there is no deputy of the king to hear you." Moreover Absalom would say, "Oh, that I were made judge in the land, and everyone who has any suit or cause would come to me; that I would give him justice."

Your take:


273. What is on your list of things you're willing to fight for?

Joshua 24:15 "And if it seems evil to you to serve the Lord, choose for yourselves this day whom you will serve, whether the gods which your fathers served that were on the other side of the River, or the gods of the Amorites, in whose land you dwell. But as for me and my house, we will serve the Lord."

James 4: 2 – 3 You lust and do not have. You murder and covet and cannot obtain. You fight and war. Yet you do not have because you do not ask. You ask and do not receive because you ask amiss, that you may spend it on your pleasures.

Your take:


274. "Old" is not measured by time, but by how we feel.

2 Kings 9:15 But King Joram had returned to Jezreel to recover from the wounds which the Syrians had inflicted on him when he fought with Hazael king of Syria. And Jehu said, "If you are so minded, let no one leave or escape from the city to go and tell it in Jezreel." So Jehu rode in a chariot and went to Jezreel, for Joram was laid up there; and Ahaziah king of Judah had come down to see Joram.

Your take:

275. Unity starts with accepting others for who they are without trying to change them.

2 Chronicles 30:12 Also the hand of God was on Judah to give them singleness of heart to obey the command of the king and the leaders, at the word of the Lord.

John 17:22 – 23 "And the glory which You gave Me I have given them, that they may be one just as We are one; I in them, and You in Me; that they may be made perfect in one, and that the world may know that You have sent Me, and have loved them as You have loved Me."

Your take:


276. God tells us that a house, much like a country, that's divided is doomed for destruction.

Daniel 2:41 - 42 Whereas you saw the feet and toes, partly of potter's clay and partly of iron, the kingdom shall be divided; yet the strength of the iron shall be in it, just as you saw the iron mixed with ceramic clay. And as the toes of the feet were partly of iron and partly of clay, so the kingdom shall be partly strong and partly fragile.

Mark 3: 24 - 25 If a kingdom is divided against itself, the kingdom cannot stand. And if Satan has risen up against himself, and is divided, he cannot stand, but has an end.

Your take:


277. Stand up for your strong faith, your family, your country, your flag and what is right in the eyes of God.

Genesis 18:19 "For I have known him, in order that he may command his children and his household after him, that they keep the way of the Lord, to do righteousness and justice, that the Lord may bring to Abraham what He has spoken to him."

Luke 20: 21 - 22 Then they asked Him, saying, "Teacher, we know that You say and teach rightly, and You do not show personal favoritism, but teach the way of God in truth; Is it lawful for us to pay taxes to Caesar or not?"

Your take:


278. There is strength in numbers, a cord of three strands is not easily broken.

Ecclesiastes 4:12 Though one may be overpowered by another, two can withstand him. And a threefold cord is not quickly broken.

Your take:


279. Always build on a solid foundation.

2 Samuel 7: 5 – 6 "Go and tell My servant David, 'Thus says the lord: "Would you build a house for Me to dwell in? For I have not dwelt in a house since the time that I brought the children of Israel up from Egypt, even to this day, but have moved about in a tent and in a tabernacle.'"

Your take:


280. Peace of mind is the lack of worry, turmoil, confusion, cares and loneliness.

Judges 3: 10 – 11 The spirit of the Lord came upon him, and he judged Israel. He went out to war, and the Lord delivered Cushan-Rishathaim king of Mesopotamia into his hand; and his hand prevailed over Cushan-Rishathaim. So the land had rest for forty years. Then Othniel the son of Kenaz died.

Your take:

281. Troubles can be your opportunity to strengthen you, and also cause you to grow.

Psalm 9: 9 – 10 The Lord will be a refuge for the oppressed, a refuge in times of trouble. And those who know Your name will put their trust in You; for You, Lord, have not forsaken those who seek You.

Your take:


282. Think on the things that are good.

Proverbs 22:11 He who loves purity of heart and has grace on his lips, the king will be his friend.

Philippians 4:8 Finally, brethren, whatever things are true, whatever things are noble, whatever things are just, whatever things are pure, whatever things are lovely, whatever things are of good report, if there is any virtue and if there is anything praiseworthy – meditate on these things.

Your take:


283. You are invited to the banquet.

Esther 5: 7 - 8 Then Esther answered and said, "My petition and request is this: If I have found favor in the sight of the king, and if it pleases the king to grant my petition, and fulfill my request, then let the king and Haman come to the banquet which I will prepare for them, and tomorrow I will do as the king has said."

Luke 12:37 Blessed are those servants whom the master, when he comes, will find watching. Assuredly, I say to you that he will gird himself and have them sit down to eat, and come and serve them

Your take:

284. That man said what?

Esther 5:12 – 13 Moreover Haman said, "Besides, Queen Esther invited no one but me to come in with the king to the banquet that she prepared; and tomorrow I am again invited by her, along with the king. Yet all this avails me nothing, so long as I see Mordecai the Jew sitting at the king's gate.

Your take:


285. When shall that be?

John 11: 24 – 26 Martha said to Him, "I know that he will rise again in the resurrection at the last day." Jesus said to her, "I am the resurrection and the life. He who believes in Me, though he may die, he shall live. And whoever lives and believes in Me shall never die. Do you believe this?"

Your take:


286. All words have meaning; some good, some bad; some soft, some hard.

Deuteronomy 6: 20 – 22 When your son asks you in time to come, saying, 'What is the meaning of the testimonies, the status, and the judgments which the Lord our God has commanded you?' Then you shall say to your son: 'We were slaves of Pharaoh in Egypt, and the Lord brought us out of Egypt with a mighty hand; and the Lord showed signs and wonders before our eyes, great and severe, against Egypt, Pharaoh, and all his household.

1 Corrinthians 4:7 For who makes you differ from another? And what do you have that you did not receive. Now if you did indeed receive it, why do you boast as if you had not received it?

Your take:

287. You have not because you failed to ask.

1 Samuel 12:23 Moreover, as for me, far be it from me that I should sin against the Lord in ceasing to pray for you; but I will teach you the good and right way.

Luke 11:9 "So I say to you, ask, and it will be given to you; seek, and you will find; knock, and it will be opened to you.

Your take:


288. So, it was so.

Genesis 15: 18 – 19 On the same day the Lord made a covenant with Abram, saying: "To your descendants I have given this land, from the river of Egypt to the great Euphrates – the Kenites, the Kenizzites, the Kadmonites, the Hittites, the Perizzites, the Rephaim, the Amorites, the Canaanites, the Girgashites and the Jebusites."

2 Kings 10:30 And the Lord said to Jehu, "Because you have done well in doing what is right in My sight, and have done to the house of Ahab all that was in My heart, your sons shall sit on the throne of Israel to the fourth generation."

Your take:


289. A gift opens doors that might not open without it.

Matthew 5: 23 – 24 Therefore if you bring your gift to the altar, and there remember that your brother has something against you, leave your gift there before the altar, and go your way. First be reconciled to your brother, and then come and offer your gift.

2 Corinthians 9: 6 – 7 But this I say: He who sows sparingly will also reap sparingly, and he who sows bountifully will also reap

bountifully. So let each one give as he purposes in his heart, not grudgingly or of necessity; for God loves a cheerful giver.

Your take:

290. Do you know the story of the speck and the plank or log?

Luke 6: 41 – 42 And why do you look at the speck in your brother's eye, but do not perceive the plank in your own eye? Or how can you say to your brother, 'Brother, let me remove the speck that is in your eye,' when you yourself do not see the plank that is in your own eye? Hypocrite! First remove the plank from your own eye, and then you will see clearly to remove the speck that is in your brother's eye.

Your take:

291. How often we are curious about something we see.

Exodus 3: 3 – 4 Then Moses said, "I will now turn aside and see this great sight, why the bush does not burn." So when the Lord saw that he turned aside to look, God called to him from the midst of the bush and said, "Moses, Moses!" And he said, "Here I am."

Psalm 24: 8 - 10 Who is this King of glory? The Lord strong and mighty. The Lord mighty in battle. Lift up your heads, O you gates! Lift up, you everlasting doors! And the King of glory shall come in. Who is this King of glory? The Lord of hosts, He is the King of glory. Selah

Your take:

292. There is only 'one first' in everything under the sun.

Genesis 1:5 God called the light Day, and the darkness He called night. So the evening and the morning were the first day.

Matthew 22: 37 – 38 Jesus said to him, "'You shall love the Lord your God with all your heart, with all your soul, and with all your mind. This is the first and great commandment.'

Your take:


293. Worry gains nothing but early aging.

Luke 10: 41 – 42 And Jesus answered and said to her, "Martha, Martha, you are worried and troubled about many things. But one thing is needed, and Mary has chosen that good part, which will not be taken away from her."

Your take:

294. A tree is known by its fruit, and by its many other benefits.

Matthew 12:33 Either make the tree good and its fruit good, or else make the tree bad and its fruit bad; for a tree is known by its fruit.

Matthew 3:10 And then now the ax is laid to the root of the trees. Therefore every tree which does not bear good fruit is cut down and thrown into the fire.

Your take:

295. Your words can either justify you or condemn you.

Matthew 12: 36 - 37 "But I say to you that for every idle word men may speak, they will give account of it in the day of judgement. For by your words you will be justified, and by your words you will be condemned."

Your take:

296. Be grateful for each brand new day you are given.

Psalm 35: 27 – 28 Let them shout for joy and be glad, who favor my righteous cause; and let them say continually, "Let the Lord be magnified, Who has pleasure in the prosperity of His servants. And my tongue shall speak of Your righteousness and of Your praise all the day long."

Your take:

297. A blank piece of paper, like a blank canvas, might be the starting point, the beginning of a hidden treasure, or in contrast a work of nonsense.

Proverbs 2: 1- 5 My son, if you receive my words, and treasure my commands within you, so that you incline your ear to wisdom, and apply your heart to understanding; yes, if you cry out for discernment, and lift up your voice for understanding, if you seek her as silver and search for her as for hidden treasures; then you will understand the fear of the Lord, and find the knowledge of God.

Isaiah 45:3 I will give you the treasures of darkness and hidden riches of secret places that you may know that I, the Lord, Who call you by your name, am the God of Israel.

Your take:


298. Daily prayer is vital to maintaining your relationship with God, and with others.

Exodus 9: 27 – 28 And Pharaoh sent and called for Moses and Aaron, and said to them, "I have sinned this time. The Lord is righteous, and my people and I are wicked. Entreat the Lord, that there may be no more mighty thundering and hail, for it is enough. I will let you go, and you shall stay no longer."

Matthew 12:35 – 37 "A good man out of the good treasure of his heart brings forth good things, and an evil man out of the evil treasure brings forth evil things. But I say to you that for every idle word men may speak, they will give account of it in the day of judgement. For by your words you will be justified, and by your words you will be condemned."

Your Take:

299. It must be one of God's favorite colors. He created a lot of things that are green.

Genesis 1: 11 – 13 Then God said, "Let the earth bring forth grass, the herb that yields seed, and fruit three that yields fruit according to its kind, whose seed is in itself, on the earth"; and it was so. And the earth brought forth grass, the herb that yields seed according to its kind, and the tree that yields fruit, whose seed is in itself according to its kind. And God saw that it was good. So the evening and the morning were the third day.

Isaiah 65: 17 – 19 "For behold, I create new heavens and a new earth; and the former shall not be remembered or come to mind. But be glad and rejoice forever in what I create; for behold, I create Jerusalem as a rejoicing, and her people a joy. I will rejoice in Jerusalem, and joy in My people; the voice of weeping shall no longer be heard in her, nor the voice of crying.

Your take:

300. It's no coincident that we have all we need available to us for survival.

Matthew 6: 7 – 8 And when you pray, do not use vain repetitions as the heathen do. For they think that they will be heard for their many words. "Therefore do not be like them. For your Father knows the things you have need of before you ask Him."

Titus 3: 13 – 14 Send Zenas the lawyer and Apollos on their journey with haste, that they may lack nothing. And let our people also learn to maintain good works, to meet urgent needs, that they may not be unfruitful.

Your take:

301. No amount of money can buy real peace, it comes when one seeks to find real peace.

Isaiah 32: 17 – 19 The work of righteousness will be peace, and the effect of righteousness, quietness and assurance forever. My people will dwell in a peaceful habitation, in secure dwellings, and in quiet resting places, though hail comes down on the forest, and the city is brought low in humiliation.

2 Chronicles 24:11 So it was, at that time, when the chest was brought to the king's official by the hand of the Levites, and when they saw that there was much money, that the king's scribe and the high priest's officer came and emptied the chest, and took it and returned it to its place. Thus they did day by day, and gathered money in abundance.

Proverbs 17:16 Why is there in the hand of a fool the purchase price of wisdom, since he has no heart for it?

Your take:

302. Daily prayers for God's will to be done, morning, noon and evening, it's important.

Exodus 9: 27 – 28 And Pharaoh sent and called for Moses and Aaron, and said to them, "I have sinned this time. The Lord is righteous, and my people and I are wicked. Entreat the Lord, that there may be no more mighty thundering and hail, for it is enough. I will let you go, and you shall stay no longer."

John 6:38 -39 For I have come down from heaven, not to do My own will, but the will of Him who sent Me, that of all He has given Me I should lose nothing, but should raise it up at the last day.

Your take:

303. Only God, through everyone who desires through much prayer, can produce true peace.

Numbers 6: 23 – 26 "Speak to Aaron and his sons, saying, 'This is the way you shall bless the children of Israel. Say to them: "The Lord bless you and keep you; The Lord make His face to shine upon you, and be gracious to you; The Lord lift up His countenance upon you, and give you peace.' "

Psalm 34: 13 – 14 Keep your tongue from evil, and your lips from speaking deceit. Depart from evil and do good; seek peace and pursue it.

Your take:


304. Words we use can either build up, or tear down, praise, or shame, exult, or reject, encourage, or discourage, etc. Take care how you use them.

Proverbs 6: 2 – 3 You are snared by the word of your mouth; you are taken by the words of your mouth. So do this, my son, and deliver yourself; for you have come into the hand of your friend; go and humble yourself; plead with your friend.

1 Corinthian 2: 15 – 16 But he who is spiritual judges all things, yet he himself is rightly judged by no one. For "Who has known the mind of the Lord that he may instruct Him?"

But we have the mind of Christ.

Your take:


305. A platform can raise you up above a crowd, or it can be a declaration of what you stand for.

Matthew 5: 1 – 4 And seeing the multitudes, He went up on a mountain, and when He was seated His disciples came to Him. Then He opened His mouth and taught them, saying: "Blessed are the poor in spirit, for theirs is the kingdom of heaven. Blessed are those who mourn, for they shall be comforted."

Luke 5: 3 - 4 Then He got into one of the boats, which was Simon's, and asked him to put out a little from the land. And He sat down and taught the multitudes from the boat. When He had stopped speaking, He said to Simon, "Launch out into the deep and let down your nets for a catch."

Your take:

306. Question, Who or what do you bow down to?

Deuteronomy 11: 16 – 17 Take heed to yourselves, lest your heart be deceived, and you turn aside and serve other gods and worship them, lest the Lord's anger be aroused against you, and He shut up the heavens so that there be no rain, and the land yield no produce, and you perish quickly from the good land which the Lord is giving you.

Romans 14: 11 – 12 For it is written: "As I live, says the Lord, every knee shall bow to Me, and every tongue shall confess to God." So then each of us shall give account of himself to God.

Your take:

307. Pride comes before a fall.

Proverbs 16: 18 – 19 Pride goes before destruction, and a haughty spirit before a fall. Better to be of a humble spirit with the lowly, than to divide the spoil with the proud.

Galatians 6: 7 – 8 Do not be deceived, God is not mocked; for whatever a man sows, that he will also reap. For he who sows to his flesh will of the flesh reap corruption, but he who sows to the Spirit will of the Spirit reap everlasting life.

Your take:

308. Can you name any other country having all the freedoms that we enjoy here?

Genesis 9: 1 - 2 So God blessed Noah and his sons, and said to them: "Be fruitful and multiply, and fill the earth. And the fear of you and the dread of you shall be on every beast of the earth, on every bird of the air, on all that move on the earth, and on all the fish of the sea. They are given into your hand."

Psalm 112: 1 – 2 Praise the Lord! Blessed is the man who fears the Lord, who delights greatly in His commandments. His descendants will be mighty on earth; the generation of the upright will be blessed.

Your take:


309. All things are possible with God.

Matthew 19: 24 – 26 "And again I say to you, it is easier for a camel to go through the eye of a needle than for a rich man to enter the kingdom of God." When His disciples heard it, they were greatly astonished, saying, "Who then can be saved?" But Jesus looked at them and said to them, "With men this is impossible, but with God all things are possible."

Your take:


310. If you need answers to your eternal questions, God's word is the best source.

2 Timothy 2: 8 – 9 Remember that Jesus Christ, of the seed of David, was raised from the dead according to my gospel, for which I suffer trouble as an evildoer, even to the point of chains; but the word of God is not chained.

2 Peter 3: 8 - 9 But, beloved, do not forget this one thing, that with the Lord one day is as a thousand years, and a thousand years as one day. The Lord is not slack concerning His promise, as some count slackness, but is longsuffering towards us, not willing that any should perish but that all should come to repentance.

Your take:

311. To make a good decision in a certain subject requires knowing all the available details.
Daniel 2: 46 – 48 The King Nebuchadnezzar fell on his face, prostrate before Daniel, and commanded that they should present an offering and incense to him. The King answered Daniel, and said. "Truly your God is the God of gods, the Lord of kings, and a revealer of secrets, since you could reveal this secret." Then the king promoted Daniel and gave him many great gifts; and he made him ruler over the whole province of Babylon, and chief administrator over all the wise men of Babylon.
Your take:

312. Your cup can be both half full or half empty depending on how you look at it.
Genesis 44: 1 – 2 And he commanded the steward of his house, saying, "Fill the men's sacks with food, as much as they can carry, and put each man's money in the mouth of his sack. Also put my cup, the silver cup, in the mouth of the sack of the youngest, and his grain money." So he did according to the word that Joseph had spoken.
Mark 9:41 "For whoever gives you a cup of water to drink in My mane, because you belong to Christ, assuredly, I say to you, he will by no means lose his reward."
Your take:

313. Your response or your attitude tells much about yourself.
Genesis 31: 2 – 3 And Jacob saw the countenance of Laban, and indeed it was not favorable toward him as before. Then the Lord said

to Jacob, "Return to the land of your fathers and to your family, and I will be with you."

1 Peter 4: 1 – 2 Therefore, since Christ suffered for us in the flesh, arm yourselves also with the same mind, for he who has suffered in the flesh has ceased from sin, that he no longer should live the rest of his time in the flesh for the lusts of men, but for the will of God.

Your take:


314. Traveling light makes for an easy and quick get-a-away, until you find out all that you didn't pack.

Matthew 23:15 "Woe to you, scribes and Pharisees, Hypocrites! For you travel land and sea to win one proselyte, and when he is won, you make him twice as much a son of hell as yourselves."

Acts 9: 3 – 4 As he journeyed he came near Damascus, and suddenly a light shone around him from heaven. Then he fell to the ground, and heard a voice saying to him, "Saul, Saul, why are you persecuting Me?"

Your take:


315. God said, "Let there be light." And I'm so glad He did.

Psalm 4:6 There are many who say, "Who will show us any good?" Lord, lift up the light of Your countenance upon us.

Isaiah 30:26 Moreover the light of the moon will be as the light of the sun, and the light of sun will be sevenfold, as the light of seven days, in the day that the Lord binds up the bruise of His people and heals the stroke of their wound.

Your take:

316. Faith is a personal thing. I don't have enough of it to believe that everything we see came from some accident or big boom.

2 Chronicles 20:20 So they rose early in the morning and went out into the wilderness to Tekoa; and as they went out, Jehoshaphat stood and said, "Hear me, O Judah and you inhabitants of Jerusalem; Believe in the Lord your God, and you shall be established; believe His prophets, and you shall prosper."

Romans 1: 16 – 17 For I am not ashamed of the gospel of Christ, for it is the power of God to salvation for everyone who believes, for the Jew first and also for the Greek. For in it the righteousness of God is revealed from faith to faith; as it is written, "The just shall live by faith."

Your take:


317. Rest when you should rest, work when you should work, and play when you can when all your other needs are met.

Psalm 55: 6 – 8 So I said, "Oh, that I had wings like a dove! I would fly away and be at rest. Indeed, I would wander far off, and remain in the wilderness." Selah. "I would hasten my escape from the windy storm and tempest."

Mark 6: 31 – 32 And He said to them, "Come aside by yourselves to a deserted place and rest a while." For there were many coming and going, and they did not even have time to eat. So they departed to a deserted place in the boat by themselves.

Your take:


318. Time waits for no one.

Joshua 23: 2 – 3 And Joshua called for all Israel, for their elders, for their heads, for their judges, and for their officers, and said to them: "I am old, advanced in age. You have seen all that the Lord your God has done to all these nations because of you, for the Lord your God is He who has fought for you."

Matthew 25: 8 – 10 And the foolish said to the wise, "Give us some of your oil, for our lamps are going out." But the wise answered, saying, "No, lest there should not be enough for us and you; but go rather to those who sell, and buy for yourselves." And while they went to buy, the bridegroom came, and those who were ready went in with him to the wedding; and the door was shut.

Your take:


319. Time flies when you are having fun.

Psalm 144: 3- 4 Lord, what is man, that You take knowledge of him? Or the son of man, that You are mindful of him? Man is like a breath; his days are like a passing shadow.

Your take:


320. If you live long enough you seem to get less done in more time.

Psalm 39: 4 - 6 "Lord, make me to know my end, and what is the measure of my days, that I may know how frail I am. Indeed, You have made my days as handbreadths, and my age is as nothing before You; certainly every man at his best state is but a vapor." Selah. "Surely every man walks about like a shadow; surely they busy themselves in vain; he heaps up riches, and does not know who will gather them."

Your take:


321. You may one day question how you ever had time to also go to work.

Haggai 1: 9 - 10 "You looked for much, but indeed it came to little; and when you brought it home, I blew it away. Why?" says the Lord of hosts. "Because of My house that is in ruins, while every one of you runs to his own house. Therefore the heavens above you withhold the dew, and the earth withholds it fruit."

Your take:


322. In time, family and friends become more important, and that's when they seem to be too busy for you.

2 Chronicles 35: 1 – 3 Now Josiah kept a Passover to the Lord in Jerusalem, and they slaughtered the Passover lambs on the fourteenth day of the first month. And he set the priests in their duties and encouraged them for the service of the house of the Lord. Then he said to the Levites who taught all Israel, who were holy to the Lord: "Put the Holy Ark in the house which Solomon the son of David, king of Israel, built. It shall no longer be a burden on your shoulders. Now serve the Lord your God and His people Israel."

Your take:


323. You wonder where all that time went.

Job 14: 1 – 2 "Man who is born of woman is of few days and full of trouble. He comes forth like a flower and fades away; he flees like a shadow and does not continue."

Your take:


324. God's reference to time is during His creation, day one through day seven.

Matthew 13: 34 – 35 All these things Jesus spoke to the multitude in parables; and without a parable He did not speak to them, that it might be fulfilled which was spoken by the prophet, saying; "I will open My mouth in parables; I will utter things kept secret from the foundation of the world."

John 17: 24 – 26 "Father, I desire that they also whom You gave Me may be with Me where I am, that they may behold My glory which You have given Me; for you loved Me before the foundation of the world. O righteous Father! The world has not known You, but I have known You; and these have known that You sent Me. And I have declared to them Your name, and will declare it, that the love with which You loved Me may be in them, and I in them."

Your take:


325. How often you say, "I can't believe what time it is."

Psalm 75: 6 – 10 For exaltation comes neither from the east nor from the west nor from the south. But God is the judge: He puts down one, and exalts another. For in the hand of the Lord there is a cup, and the wine is red; it is fully mixed, and He pours it out; surely its dregs shall all the wicked of the earth drain and drink down. But I will declare forever, I will sing praises of the God of Jacob. "All the horns of the wicked I will cut off, but the horns of the righteous shall be exalted."

Your take:


326. You should schedule your time so you fit in all that's important to you.

> Psalm 146: 5 – 8 Happy is he who has the God of Jacob for his help, whose hope is in
>
> Lord his God, Who made heaven and earth, the sea, and all that is in them; Who keeps

truth forever, Who executes justice for the oppressed, Who give food to the hungry. The

Lord gives freedom to the prisoners. The Lord opens the eyes of the blind; the Lord

raises those who are bowed down; the Lord loves the righteous.

Your take:


327. The Lord promised to one day come back for all who believe in Him as their Lord and savior.
   Mark 13: 35 -37 "Watch therefore, for you do not know when the Master of the house is coming – in the evening, at midnight, at the crowing of the rooster, or in the morning- lest, coming suddenly, He find you sleeping. And what I say to you, I say to all; 'Watch!'"
   Luke 21: 34 – 36 "But take heed to yourselves, lest you hearts be weighed down with carousing, drunkenness, and care of this life, and that Day come on you unexpectedly. For it will come as a snare on all those who dwell on the face of the whole earth. Watch therefore, and pray always that you may be counted worthy to escape all these things that will come to pass, and to stand before the Son of Man."
   Your take:


328. Kill the sin in your life before it kills you.
   Genesis 42: 22 – 24 And Reuben answered them, saying, "Did I not speak to you, saying, 'Do not sin against the boy, and you would not listen? Therefore behold, his blood is now required of us." But they did not know that Joseph understood them, for he spoke to them through an interpreter. And he turned himself away from them and

wept. Then he returned to them again, and talked with them. And he took Simeon from them and bound him before their eyes.

Psalm 106: 42 – 45 Their enemies also oppressed them, and they were brought into subjection under their hand. Many times He delivered them; but they rebelled in their counsel, and were brought low for their iniquity. Nevertheless He regarded their affliction, when He heard their cry; and for their sake He remembered His covenant, and relented according to the multitude of His mercies.

Your take:


329. Strive for a greater affection for things good to replace those that are bad.

Ecclesiastes 2:26 For God gives wisdom and knowledge and joy to a man who is good in His sight; but to the sinner He gives the work of gathering and collecting, that he may give to him who is good before God. This also is vanity and grasping for the wind.

Acts 24:16 "This being so, I myself always strive to have a conscience without offense toward God and men."

Your take:


330. Invest in things that will have lasting value for you and yours.

Hebrews 10: 32 – 34 But recall the former days in which, after you were illuminated, you endured a great struggle with sufferings: partly while you were made a spectacle both by reproaches and tribulations, and partly while you became companions of those who were so treated; for you had compassion on me in my chains, and joyfully accepted the plundering of your goods, knowing that you have a better and an enduring possession for yourselves in heaven.

Your take:

331. Humility is an asset, while pride can cause you to fall.

1 Kings 21: 28 – 29 And the Word of the Lord came to Elijah the Tishbite, saying,

"See how Ahab has humbled himself before Me? Because he has humbled himself before Me, I will not bring the calamity in his days. In the days of his son I will bring the calamity on his house."

Isaiah 5: 15 – 16 People shall be brought down, each man shall be humbled, and the eyes of the lofty shall be humbled. But the Lord of hosts shall be exalted in judgment, and God who is holy shall be hallowed in righteousness.

Your take:


332. Life cycle is no accident. It's a divine plan, you're born; you live and work; you have a family and one day your life here on earth will end. Fruitfully work during that time.

2 Peter 1: 2 – 3 Grace and peace be multiplied to you in the knowledge of God and of Jesus our Lord, as His divine power has given to us all things that pertain to life and godliness, through the knowledge of Him who called us by glory and virtue, by which have been given to us exceedingly great and precious promises, that through these you may be partakers of the divine nature, having escaped the corruption that is in the world through lust.

Your take:


333. Say only what you mean, and mean only what you say.

Psalm 15: 2 – 4 He who walks uprightly, and works righteousness, and speaks the truth in his heart; he who does not backbite with his tongue, nor does evil to his neighbor, nor does he take up a reproach against his friend; in whose eyes a vile person is despised, but he honors those who fear the Lord; he who swears to his own hurt and does not change; he who does not put out his money at usury, nor does he take a bribe against the innocent. He who does these things shall never be moved.

Matthew 12: 6 – 8 "'Yet I say to you that in this place there is One greater than the temple. But if you had known what this means, 'I desire mercy and not sacrifice,' you would not have condemned the guiltless. For the Son of Man is Lord even of the Sabbath."

Your take:


334. Excuses are easier to find than solutions, but never best.

Luke 14: 18 – 20 But they all with one accord began to make excuses. The first said to him, "I have bought a piece of ground, and I must go and see it. I ask you to have me excused." And another said, "I have bought five yoke of oxen, and I am going to test them. I ask you to have me excused." Still another said, "I have married a wife, and therefore I cannot come."

Romans 1: 20 – 21 For since the creation of the world His invisible attributes are clearly seen, being understood by the things that are made, even His eternal power and Godhead, so that they are without excuse, because, although they knew God, they did not glorify Him as God, nor were thankful, but became futile in their thoughts, and their foolish hearts were darkened.

Your take:


335. Be willing to speak up, its better, and the best chance of preserving what's important.

Matthew 6: 31 – 33 "Therefore do not worry, saying, 'What shall we eat?' or 'What shall we drink, or what shall we wear?' For after all these things the Gentiles seek. For your heavenly Father knows that you need all these things. But seek first the kingdom of God and His righteousness, and all these things shall be added to you."

Philippians 1:18 What then? Only that in every way, whether in pretense or in truth, Christ is preached; and in this I rejoice, yes and will rejoice.

Your take:


336. If you fail to speak up you might lose the right to complain later when things don't go as you want.

Isaiah 29: 22 – 24 Therefore thus says the Lord, who redeemed Abraham, concerning the house of Jacob; "Jacob shall not now be ashamed, nor shall his face now grow pale; but when he sees his children, the work of My hands, in his midst, they will hallow My name, and hallow the Holy One of Jacob, and fear the God of Israel. These also who erred in spirit will come to understanding, and those who complained will learn doctrine."

Philippians 2: 14 - 16 Do all things without complaining and disputing, that you may become blameless and harmless, children of God without fault in the midst of a crooked and perverse generation, among whom you shine as lights in the world, holding fast the word of life, so that I may rejoice in the day of Christ that I have not run in vain or labored in vain.

Your take:


337. Because of the brave who gave their all, we live in the land and family of freedom. Matthew 27: 49 – 50 The rest said, "Let Him alone; let us see if Elijah will come to save Him." And Jesus cried out again with a loud voice, and yielded up His spirit.

John 1: 12 – 13 But as many as received Him, to them He gave the right to become children of God, to those who believe in His name: who were born, not of blood, nor of the will of the flesh, nor of the will of man, but of God.

Your take:

338. Freedom is beyond price, and given only by the unselfish sacrifices made.

Isaiah 45: 11 – 13 Thus says the Lord, the Holy One of Israel, and his Maker; "Ask Me of things to come concerning My sons; and concerning the work of My hands, you command Me. I have made the earth, and created man on it. I- My hands – stretched out the heavens, and all their host I have commanded. I have raised him up in righteousness, and I will direct all his ways; he shall build My city and let My exiles go free, not for price nor reward," says the Lord of hosts.

Your take:

339. Fire can be both a benefit and a threat to you.

Exodus 40: 36 – 37 Whenever the cloud was taken up from above the tabernacle, the children of Israel would go onward in all their journeys. But, if the cloud was not taken up, then they did not journey till the day that it was taken up. For the cloud of the Lord was above the tabernacle by day, and fire was over it by night, in the sight of all the house of Israel, throughout all their journeys.

Psalm 83: 13 – 15 O my God, make them like the whirling dust, like the chaff before the wind! As the fire burns the woods, and as the flame set the mountains on fire, so pursue them with your tempest, and frighten them with Your storm.

Your take:

340. An explanation by the late Sir Winston Churchill for the difference between "Capitalism and socialism. Capitalism is an uneven, open experience where everyone has the freedom to seek prosperity, while Socialism is an even, oppressive experiment in poverty for all but a very few.

Judges 16: 20 – 21 And she said, "The Philistines are upon you, Samson!" So he awoke from his sleep and said, "I will go out as before, at other times, and shake myself free!" But he did not know that the Lord had departed from him. Then the Philistines took him and put out his eyes, and brought him down to Gaza. They bound him with bronze fetters, and he became a grinder in the prison.

1 Peter 2: 15 – 17 For this is the will of God, that by doing good you may put to silence the ignorance of foolish men – as free, yet not using liberty as a cloak for vice, but as bondservants of God. Honor all people. Love the brotherhood. Fear God. Honor the King.

Your take:


341. We 'The People' should strive to be 'United' and 'Universal', along with being 'Unique' at the same time.

1 Corinthians 1: 10 – 11 Now I plead with you, brethren, by the name of our Lord Jesus Christ, that you all speak the same thing, and that there be no divisions among you, but that you be perfectly joined together in the same mind and the same judgment.

Your take:


342. Whatever happened to 'peacefully' agreeing to disagree?

1 Kings 20: 9 – 10 Therefore he said to the messengers of Ben-Hadad, "Tell my lord the king, 'All that you sent for to your

servant the first time I will do, but this thing I cannot do.'" And the messengers departed and brought back word to him. Then Ben-Hadad sent to him and said, "The gods do so to me, and more also, if enough dust is left of Samaria for a handful for each of the people who follow me."

Your take:


343. Your real personal story belongs only to you and to God.

1 John 3: 18 – 19 My little children, let us not love in word or in tongue, but in deed and in truth. And by this we know that we are of the truth, and shall assure our hearts before him.

Your take:


344. It's of no coincidence that we have available everything we need to survive.

Matthew 7: 7 – 11 "Ask, and it will be given to you; seek and you will find; knock, and it will be opened to you. For everyone who asks receives, and he who seek finds, and to him who knocks it will be opened. Or what man is there among you who, if his son asks for bread, will give him a stone? Or if he asks for a fish, will he give him a serpent? If you then, being evil, know how to give good gifts to your children, how much more will your Father who is in heaven give good things to those who ask Him!"

Your take:


345. No amount of peace can be bought. It comes only when you decide to go to the real only source of peace.

1 Kings 1: 29 – 30 And the king took an oath and said, "As the Lord lives, who has redeemed my life from every distress, just as I swore

to you by the Lord God of Israel, saying, 'Assuredly Solomon your son shall be king after me, and he shall sit on my throne in my place, so I certainly will do this day.'"

Isaiah 59:8 The way of peace they have not known, and there is no justice in their ways; they have made themselves crooked paths; whoever takes that way shall not know peace.

Luke 14: 31 – 32 Or what king, going to make war against another king, does not sit down first and consider whether he is able with ten thousand to meet him who comes against him with twenty thousand? Or else, while the other is still a great way off, he send a delegation and asks conditions of peace.

Your take:


346. Lack of order produces chaos.

Proverbs 28:2 Because of the transgression of a land, many are its princes; but by a man of understanding and knowledge right will be prolonged.

Psalm 82:5 They do not know, nor do they understand; They walk about in darkness; all the foundations of the earth are unstable.

Your take:


347. A lack of calm brings distress.

Psalm 107: 10 – 12 Those who sat in darkness and in the shadows of death, bound in affliction and irons because they rebelled against the words of God, and despised the counsel of the Most High, therefore He brought down their heart with labor; they fell down and there was none to help.

Mark 4:39 - 41 Then He arose and rebuked the wind, and said to the sea, "Peace, be still!" And the wind ceased and there was a great calm. But He said to them, "Why are you so fearful? How is it that you have no faith?" And they feared exceedingly, and said to one another, "Who can this be, that even the wind and the sea obey Him?"

Your take:

348. A lack of rain results in drought conditions.

Deuteronomy 28:24 The Lord will change the rain of your land to powder and dust; from the heaven it shall come down on you until you are destroyed.

Haggai 1:11 "For I called for a drought on the land and the mountains, on the grain and the new wine and the oil, on whatever the ground brings forth, on men and livestock, and on the labor of your hands."

Your take:

349. A lack of hope means hopelessness.

Proverbs 11:7 – 8 When a wicked man dies, his expectation will perish, and the hope of the unjust perishes. And the hope of the unjust perishes. The righteous is delivered from trouble, and it comes to the wicked instead.

Proverbs 24:20 – 22 For there will be no prospect for the evil man; the lamp of the wicked will be put out. My son, fear the Lord and the king; do not associate with those given to change; for their calamity will rise suddenly, and who knows the ruin those two can bring?

Your take:

350. A lack of peace translates as anxiousness.

Proverbs 12:25 – 26 Anxiety in the heart of man causes depression, but a good word makes it glad. The righteous should choose his friends carefully, for the way of the wicked leads them astray.

Philippians 4:6 Be anxious for nothing, but in everything by prayer and supplication, with thanksgiving, let your requests be made known to God; and the peace of God, which surpasses all understanding, will guard your hearts and minds through Christ Jesus.

Your take:


351. A lack of light makes darkness.

Psalm 91: 5 – 6 You shall not be afraid of the terror by night, nor of the arrow that flies by day, nor of the pestilence that walks in darkness, nor of the destruction that lays waste at noonday.

Proverbs 20:20 Whoever curses his father or his mother, his lamp will be put out in deep darkness.

Your take:


352. Thank God for the light.

Genesis 1: 3 – 4 Then God said, "Let there be light"; and there was light. And God saw the light, that it was good; and He divided the light from the darkness.

John 1: 6 – 8 There was a man sent from God, whose name was John. This man came for a witness, to bear witness of the light that all through him might believe. He was not that light, but was sent to bear witness of that Light.

Genesis 1: 17 – 19 God set them in the firmament of the heavens to give light on the earth, and to rule over the day and over the night, and to divide the light from the darkness. And God saw that it was good. So the evening and the morning were the fourth day.

Your take:


353. God created flowers for His pleasure and for yours and mine as well.

Genesis 1: 11 – 13 Then God said, "Let the earth bring forth grass, the herb that yields seed, and the fruit tree that yields fruit according to its kind, whose seed is in itself, on the earth"; and it was so. And the earth brought fourth grass, the herb that yields seed according to it kind, and the tree that yields fruit, whose seed is in itself according to its kind. And God saw that it was good. So the evening and the morning were the third day.

Isaiah 40: 27 – 28 Why do you say, O Jacob, and speak, O Israel: "My way is hidden from the Lord, and my just claim is passed over by my God"? Have you not known? Have you not heard? The everlasting God, the Lord, the Creator of the ends of the earth, neither faints nor is weary. His understanding is unsearchable.

Your take:


354. The difference between 'Theory and Truth', theory is an educated guess, while truth is total proven facts with no room for doubt.

John 18:37 Pilate therefore said to Him, "Are you a king then?" Jesus answered, "You say righty that I am a king. For this cause I was born, and for this cause I have come into the world, that I should bear witness to the truth. Everyone who is of the truth hears My voice."

Acts 2:36 "Therefore let all the house of Israel know assuredly that God has made this Jesus, whom you crucified, both Lord and Christ."

Your Take


355. Truth, In Genesis chapter one God told us He created the heaven and earth, but Darwin's theory, speculates it all came about by some big boom, or accident.

John 1: 1 – 5 In the beginning was the Word, and the Word was with god, and the Word was God. He was in the beginning with God. All things were made through Him, and without Him nothing was made that was made. In Him was life, and the life was the light of men. And the light shines in the darkness, and the darkness did not comprehend it.

Your take:

356. Integrity, meaning wisdom, honesty, uprighteous, openness, and candidness make for a great model for us to live by.

Psalm 78:72 So he shepherded them according to the integrity of his heart, and guided them by the skillfulness of his hands.

Psalm 94:15 But judgment will return to righteousness, and all the upright in heart will follow it.

Proverbs 11:3 The integrity of the upright will guide them, but the perversity of the unfaithful will destroy them.

Your take:

357. Strive, within reason, to be agreeable with your family, neighbors and friends.

Daniel 1:14 – 15 So he consented with them in this matter, and tested them ten days. And at the end of ten days their features appeared better and fatter in flesh than all the young men who ate the portion of the king's delicacies.

Acts 15:28 - 29 For it seemed good to the Holy Spirit, and to us, to lay upon you no greater burden than these necessary things: that you abstain from things offered to idols, from blood, from things strangled, and from sexual immortality. If you keep yourself from these, you will do well.

Your take:

358. You may need 'daily bread', spiritual bread that is. Here's where to find it.

Reading from John 1:1 through Revelation 22:21 gives you the whole story of who Jesus is and what He has done for all of mankind worldwide. He never forces anyone to accept Him, but only shows love and an open door to all to come to him.

Your take:


359. The Bible says a day is coming when followers of Christ will have no more pain, no more tears and no more sorrow.

Isaiah 35:10 And the ransomed of the Lord shall return, and come to Zion with singing, with everlasting joy on their heads. They shall obtain joy and gladness, and sorrow and sighing shall flee away.

Jeremiah 31:13 "Then shall the virgin rejoice in the dance, and the young men and the old together; for I will turn their mourning to joy, will comfort them, and make them rejoice rather than sorrow. I will satiate the soul of the priests with abundance, and My people shall be satisfied with My goodness," says the Lord.

Your take:


360. Gaining interest on your funds is better than paying interest for their funds.

Exodus 22: 25 – 26 "If you lend money to any of My people who are poor among you, you shall not be like the moneylender to him; you shall not charge him interest. If you ever take you neighbor's garment as a pledge, you shall return it to him before the sun goes down."

Luke 19:23 "Why then did you not put my money in the bank, that at my coming I might have collected it with interest?"

Your take:

361. God gave us a free gift that cost us nothing, but cost Him everything.

John 4: 13 – 14 Jesus answered and said to her, "Whoever drinks of this water will thirst again, but whoever drinks of the water that I shall give him will never thirst. But the water that I shall give him will become in him a fountain of water springing up into everlasting life."

Romans 6:23 For the wages of sin is death, but the gift of God is eternal life in Christ Jesus our Lord.

Your take:


362. Webster calls home, 1. One's residence. 2. A social unit formed by family living together. 3. A congenial environment. 4. A place of origin. 5. The goal in various games.

Ruth 1:16 But Ruth said: "Entreat me not to leave you, or to turn back from following after you; for wherever you go, I will go; and wherever you lodge, I will lodge; your people shall be my people, and your God, my God."

Matthew 10:13 "If the household is worthy, let your peace come upon it. But if it is not worthy, let your peace return to you."

Your take:


363. Mending a fence might be easier than mending a relationship.

Genesis 35:1 Then God said to Jacob, "Arise, go up to Bethel and dwell there; and make an altar there to God, Who appeared to you when you fled from the face of Esau your brother."

Ecclesiastes 3: 7 – 8 A time to tear, and a time to sew; a time to keep silence, and a time to speak; a time to love, and a time to hate; a time of war, and a time of peace.

Your take:


364: Seek after only those things that are worthwhile.

Ecclesiastes 2: 10 – 11 Whatever my eyes desired I did not keep from them. I did not withhold my heart from any pleasure, for my heart rejoiced in all my labor; and this was my reward from all my labor. Then I looked on all the works that my hands had done and on the labor in which I had toiled; and indeed all was vanity and grasping for the wind.

Hebrew 3: 1 – 3 Therefore, holy brethren, partakers of the heavenly calling, consider the Apostle and High priest of our confession, Christ Jesus, who was faithful to Him who appointed Him, as Moses also was faithful in all His house. For this one has been counted worthy of more glory than Moses, inasmuch as He who built the house has more honor than the house.

Your take:


365. Never again!

Genesis 9: 11 – 13 "Thus I establish My covenant with you: Never again shall all flesh be cut off by the waters of the flood; never again shall there be a flood to destroy the earth." And God said, "This is the sign of the covenant which I make between Me and you, and every living creature that is with you, for perpetual generations: I set My rainbow in the cloud, and it shall be for the sign of the covenant between Me and the earth.

Matthew 24: 38 – 39 For as in the days before the flood, they were eating and drinking, marrying and giving in marriage, until the day that Noah entered the ark, and did not know until the flood came and took them all away, so also will the coming of the Son of Man be.

Your take:

### Leap year question:

366. Watch therefore, for you do not know what hour your Lord is coming.

Genesis 19: 12 – 13 Then the men said to Lot, "Have you anyone else here? Son-in-law, you sons, your daughters, and whomever you have in the city – take them out of this place! For we will destroy this place, because the outcry against them has grown great before the face of the Lord, and the Lord has sent us to destroy it."

Luke 17: 31 – 32 "In that day, he who is on the housetop, and his goods are in the house, let him not come down to take them away. And likewise the one who is in the field, let him not turn back. Remember Lot's wife."

Your take:


A. The most important question we all should consider is, where will you and I decide to spend eternity? It's our decision to make!

Ephesian 6: 14 – 20 Stand therefore, having girded your waist with truth, having put on the breastplate of righteousness, and having shod your feet with the preparation of the gospel of peace; above all, taking the shield of faith with which you will be able to quench all the fiery darts of the wicked one. And take the helmet of salvation, and the sword of the Spirit, which is the word of God; praying always with all prayer and supplication in the Spirit, being watchful to this end with all perseverance and supplication for all the saints – and for me, that utterance may be given to me, that I may open my mouth boldly to make known the mystery of the gospel, for which I am an ambassador in chains; that in it I may speak boldly, as I ought to speak.

Your take:

B. Your question, who will be taken to be forever with the Lord and who will be separated out?

Read in the Holy Bible, Matthew, chapter 25, verses 1 through 46. It explains clearly by The Lord Jesus in parables, the story of the talents; of the ten virgins; five wise and five foolish; also, along with the wise and the foolish, the wise who took care of the poor, and the foolish who did not.

Your Take:

> C. If you want to find answers to your question: Are we close to the (End of The Age?)

Go to the word of God, read Matthew, Chapter 24, verses 3 through 51.

Your Take:

May the Lord Jesus Christ become more and more a part of your life as you continue to study all about Him and all that He has done for each one of us.

**God Bless you one and all!!**

To Read some of my Christian based, fiction books, as well as, my other non-fiction books, see the list below:

**(Fiction:) FASCINATION WITH LIFE SERIES:**

The longest Five Minutes, book # 1
The Daughter, book # 2
Angela the Daughter, book # 3
Modern Day Cowboy, book # 4

**(Fiction:) SURVIVAL SERIES:**
Survival Series Collection I, three short stories.
Survival Series Collection II, three short stories.

**STAND-ALONE - Fiction Novels:**
Sugarhill Families
Captain Sam
The Bridge so Long
Traveling Light

**Nonfiction:** (Available in February 2021)
Why? Are We Crumbling from Within? =
(A story about the condition of our Nation.)

**This book Title**: Daily Devotional with the Inspired Word of God

**with a subtitle**: A 365 day devotional with Patterns Truths

and Inspirations.

# Don't miss out!

Visit the website below and you can sign up to receive emails whenever J. Gordon Monson publishes a new book. There's no charge and no obligation.

https://books2read.com/r/B-A-YEBG-UNITB

BOOKS 2 READ

Connecting independent readers to independent writers.

CPSIA information can be obtained
at www.ICGtesting.com
Printed in the USA
JSHW080152030423
39813JS00003B/163